ADVANCE PRAISE FOR
ONE BASE AT A TIME

"Dave Mellor, operating on a canvas of grass and dirt, has transformed our field at Fenway Park into a shimmering work of art for nearly two decades. Now Boston's greatest gardener shares his personal story of facing and ultimately overcoming PTSD, one that should inspire hope in all who read it."

—SAM KENNEDY, Boston Red Sox President and CEO

"David's book is a must-read, inspiration for anyone facing challenges… which is all of us! His childhood dream of playing Major League Baseball was crushed after several devastating, physical attacks that left him with non-combat related PTSD. But he persevered 'One Base at a Time' with a true 'Never-Quit' attitude and now runs the team responsible for the most professional grounds keeping at the holiest of baseball cathedrals: Fenway Park. This is a true story of how to reach your goal while realizing that roadblocks are only detours."

—ROBERT J. O'NEILL, Former Navy SEAL

"Dave Mellor brings to light the multifaceted challenges encountered by people struggling to overcome the physical and mental injuries of trauma. A truly inspiring story of one man's efforts to overcome significant adversity."

—JACK HAMMOND, Brigadier General USA Ret., Executive Director, Home Base,
A Red Sox Foundation and Massachusetts General Hospital Program

"David has an amazing life story about overcoming adversity! He leads by example and is extremely motivating showing that your emotional/mental strength needs as much conditioning as your physical strength! I also learned from the book, 'Life is good because you decided to make it that way! If you want to make a positive impact, have a positive life!'"

—PETER HOFFMANN, Commander, 126 Air Refueling Squadron, Lt Col (Ret)

"The Comeback Kid. A story of one man, his family, and how to overcome trauma. Dave Mellor shows us how post-traumatic stress can become post-traumatic growth—a must read for all who face adversity and need an example for how to regain our lives."

—MICHAEL ALLARD, Chief Operating Officer, Home Base: A Red Sox
Foundation and Massachusetts General Hospital Program

"The reality is that PTSD is not only found in men and women returning from battle. It rears its ugly head in all aspects of our society, from those abused as children to people scarred from having observed a terrible crime. David is a patient of mine who tells here his story of multiple terrible traumas. He had over 40 surgeries, developed a disabling chronic pain syndrome, and lives with PTSD from all of the experiences. I was his neurosurgeon treating his chronic pain and heard firsthand what these events had done to him, but I also saw evidence of how he had resurrected his life, becoming a highly-functioning member of society, directing the Fenway Park groundscrew (one of the best in baseball), having a family, and now having the courage to help others out of their own PTSD darkness. If you have PTSD or know someone who does, read this book!"

—JEFF ARLE, MD, PhD, Neurosurgeon, Harvard Medical School

"I could not put it down! As a major league crew chief my job is to get the game in! I rely heavily on the grounds crew in each stadium, particularly the head groundskeeper. There are only thirty people who do this job, and they are all excellent. David Mellor is a man who stands out in a field of excellence. What amazes me is, despite everything life has thrown at David, he has emerged at the top of his profession. This man has not only gotten up from the mat numerous times, he has won the fight by a unanimous decision! This book has inspired me to keep the faith, and keep fighting the good fight. I admire the courage David has to speak about his struggles, I know it will help many people who are suffering. Baseball can be a ruthless game with very little forgiveness. You have to get the job done no matter what. David not only gets the job done, he gets it done the right way! When I make a call in a game that goes against your team, you probably don't like it. I am telling you to read this book, I know this is a call that no one will argue with!"

—Ted Barrett, Major League Umpire, Crew Chief #65

"I know David, not only as one of the best, most trusted groundskeepers in Major League Baseball, but more importantly, someone who has a deep compassion for people. Discussing my own history with concussions, David and I formed a bond, so I know firsthand his desire to help others. This book does just that, by telling his very personal story and relating his experiences...the setbacks and disappointments, the embarrassment, fear and guilt, withdrawing from family and friends, and finally, the courage and strength to seek help. If you have PTSD or think you might, read David's journey. You may find it to be a lot like yours..."

—Dale Scott, thirty-two-year MLB Umpire (retired 2018) and sixteen-year crew chief

"As a psychologist who works with clients suffering from PTSD, I was immediately struck by the personal aspect of David's story. How tragic to have your dreams crushed in such a cruel manner. My other reaction was a bit more selfish. I realized that I could share this inspiring story with my own clients: 'You say that you're feeling a little embarrassed to admit that you're not coping well with this trauma? You're thinking that "a tougher person should be able to handle this?" Are you a Red Sox fan? Let me tell you the story of David Mellor, Head Groundskeeper for Fenway Park.'

"I wrote to David and told him how thankful I was that he had decided to share his story. I said that I was sure I'd be able to use it to help others realize that they were acting like any other human being would in their shoes. 'You are having a NORMAL reaction to a very ABNORMAL situation; welcome to the human race.' David did a big favor for professionals like myself, and for anyone who is struggling to overcome a trauma."

—Paul Shiebler, Psy.D, Licensed Psychologist

ONE BASE AT A TIME

To Pamela –

HOW I SURVIVED PTSD
AND FOUND MY FIELD OF DREAMS

*Anything is possible
One Base at a Time!!!*

DAVID R. MELLOR

Senior Director of Grounds, Boston Red Sox

David R. Mellor

Post Hill
PRESS

A POST HILL PRESS BOOK

One Base at a Time:
How I Survived PTSD and Found My Field of Dreams
© 2019 by David R. Mellor
All Rights Reserved

ISBN: 978-1-64293-252-2
ISBN (eBook): 978-1-64293-253-9

Cover photo by Billie Weiss
Interior design and composition by Greg Johnson/Textbook Perfect

No part of this book may be reproduced, stored in a retrieval system,
or transmitted by any means without the written permission of the
author and publisher.

Post Hill Press
New York • Nashville
posthillpress.com

Published in the United States of America

DEDICATION

To everyone who is facing challenges and dealing with traumas. You are not alone. Don't give up. It's not easy or pretty but, with treatment, you too can heal. Please remember that you have the power to choose to believe in yourself, and you can start by taking it one step at a time, *One Base at a Time*.

To the double-amputee gentleman I saw in physical therapy years ago: Your infectious positive attitude and never-give-up spirit has inspired me every day. Thank you. A positive attitude is a powerful force and we can all learn from your glowing example.

Foreword

By Buster Olney

*T*he moments before each broadcast present a fight against adrenaline and, through the years, I've learned to ease that tension by distracting myself from the business at hand. A conversation with the cameraman about his hometown, or maybe a friendly shout to a front-row fan wearing an interesting shirt, or a quick chat with a player walking by. Anything to dissipate the logjam of information that caroms in your mind as you wait for the producer's countdown to start the show.

About a decade ago, we had an Opening Day broadcast in Fenway Park, and we were about five minutes to air when I saw a man carrying a rake—Dave Mellor, the head groundskeeper of the oldest and most unusual major-league ballpark in America. We made eye contact and I asked him a simple question: "How did you get into this business?"

Dave smiled and paused, and I could tell he was assessing the question of where to start in the back story, and then he detailed one of the most incredible journeys I've ever heard since I began working as a reporter.

A love and passion for baseball—for playing baseball. A terrible, improbable accident. Many surgeries. The Thanksgiving Day arrival of a letter from a legend. The desire to work outside, in the grass and dirt, under the sun. Incredibly, another awful accident, even more improbable than the first. A long road back. A dream realized. More suffering, before a life-changing diagnosis.

In those few minutes that Dave outlined his lifetime, I knew instantly that this was a story that needs to be told, a story that needs to be heard—not just by baseball fans or patrons of Fenway Park, but by anyone facing challenges.

We aired an E:60 piece on Dave for ESPN, but an unfortunate aspect of television is the time management. In order to save a few seconds here or there, important and nuanced details must be left behind. I am so glad that Dave tells the complete version here, from which others can glean the most important lessons and the best kind of inspiration.

Prologue

ONE DAY AT FENWAY

*T*he morning of Sunday, May 22, 2011 was cloudy and cool, almost foggy. As groundskeeper for the Red Sox and Fenway Park, checking the weather is often the first and last thing I do each day. It had been warm the day before but, even though the team was scheduled to play the Cubs later that evening, I was glad the weather had turned a little cooler and there wasn't much chance of rain. The runners would appreciate that.

I spend a lot of time at the ballpark during the baseball season but, on this day, something just as important as a ballgame required the attention of my crew.

Every year, Massachusetts General Hospital holds the Run to Home Base, a fundraiser for the Home Base program. Founded in 2009 and spearheaded by Chairman Tom Werner, Home Base was inspired by a visit the Red Sox made to Walter Reed Army Hospital in the spring of 2008. The program is a partnership of the Red Sox Foundation and Mass General. Their experts work with service members, veterans, and their families, particularly those affected by Post Traumatic Stress Disorder (PTSD) and Traumatic Brain Injury

(TBI). It's an amazing program that has provided care and support to over twenty-one thousand veterans and families and training to more than seventy-three thousand clinicians around the country. Veterans, their friends, and members of their families take part in the run along with various people who raised money in support of the program.

Prior to the run, as with many other non-baseball events at Fenway, we put modular flooring down on the grass so that foot traffic doesn't damage the turf. After crossing home plate, the runners are greeted by a group of military generals who congratulate each one. Afterwards, we pull the flooring up and make Fenway Park, the most beautiful ballpark in the country, look like a ballpark again.

On this day, hundreds of runners ended their nine-kilometer run on the warning track in front of the Green Monster. Afterwards, they walk to home plate, meet the generals and Red Sox Executives, and have their pictures taken. Many are thrilled, not just by finishing the run, but by being able to walk on the same field that so many great Red Sox players have played on over the years—Babe Ruth, Ted Williams, Carl Yastrzemski, David Ortiz. I stood nearby. It gave me goosebumps to watch so many people smiling as they stepped on the plate (some even bent down to kiss it), many of them fulfilling lifelong dreams. And for many of those who have lived with either PTSD or TBI, crossing home plate can be even more powerful, symbolizing how much they have accomplished since beginning treatment after their trauma. More than once, I wiped away tears.

I have been groundskeeper at Fenway since 2001 and met a lot of wonderful people during that time. I knew some of the runners. And, because I spend so much time at the ballpark, my face is familiar to many fans. Some came over and introduced themselves, so I spent much of the morning chatting with old and new friends.

I was on the infield grass when I saw my friend, Lucas, waving to me from beyond third base. We had met the previous season when he had come to Fenway to throw out the first pitch on May 2, 2011, the day after Osama Bin Laden was killed. Lucas was an Army Ranger who had been deployed five times. He ran the race in his fatigues while carrying an eighty-pound backpack. I was honored that he remembered me and excited to see him again. After we said hello and chatted for a moment, he told me about his best friend, Jessy.

Jessy loved Fenway. When he was in Afghanistan, he told everyone that, when he returned to the States, he planned to take his girlfriend to the ballpark to ask her to marry him. That's the kind of place Fenway is for so many baseball fans. It's in their hearts. It feels like a home. While on his last mission in Iraq, just before he was scheduled to return home, Jessy's Black Hawk helicopter was shot down and he was killed.

Lucas removed a black metal bracelet from his wrist and handed it to me. The engraved lettering read "CPL JESSY POLLARD 25th Infantry Division/HHC 2-35 22 August 2007 Iraq" along with a flag insignia. He told me it was a KIA bracelet—Killed in Action. Lucas said he would be honored if I would wear it for Jessy. Then he told me Jessy would look after me, care for me, and give me strength, especially any time I needed a little extra support.

I had never met Jessy, but Lucas somehow knew that I needed support just as much as anyone else. Although I never served in the military and was never shot down or felt the concussion from a roadside bomb or seen my best friend killed, Lucas knew I shared something with so many others in Fenway Park that day. Since 1981, I have suffered from PTSD.

Lucas and I shared a powerful hug. I slipped the bracelet onto my wrist, and it has remained there ever since.

After we said goodbye and he walked off, I couldn't believe how much our short visit and his gift touched me. As I stood there contemplating the many veterans and their families, I thought back to how powerfully my PTSD had affected both me and my family, and how long it had taken to realize that PTSD is not something caused only by war, but by all sorts of traumatic events. Still, I felt some guilt over the fact that the soldiers' traumas came in service to their country, while mine was the result of an accident. And I was ashamed that I hadn't spoken up sooner, to become a better husband and a better father and to help others. My heart ached, knowing how much pain I had caused, while also trying to imagine how much pain the soldiers and their families had gone through. Nevertheless, I was beginning to understand just how difficult it was for anyone to face PTSD and was becoming more determined than ever not to hide my journey and pain if I could help another person. My PTSD had dominated my life for so long that I knew many of the struggles the military veterans and their families faced. I felt blessed I had recently begun treatment and prayed that everyone who suffers PTSD could find help and support. I don't want any person on earth to suffer in silence like I did, or my loved ones had.

Tears ran down my face as I made my way off the field to my office. I called my wife, Denise, to tell her how much I loved her and to thank her again for her love and support. Then I told her about Lucas and Jessy and cried some more as I thought of all those who were at the run who might be affected by PTSD. Hundreds ran that day, and I knew there were hundreds and thousands more, all over the world, that do not yet recognize the cause of their own suffering.

Before I received treatment, I probably would have hidden away after such an emotional experience or pretended I was unaffected. Now, after my call to Denise, I gathered myself and went back out to the field. Although I was still emotional, the event was coming to an end. My staff and I started taking off the flooring and removing other items from the field, so we could prepare it for the game later that evening.

As I stood on home plate, Bob, a buddy of mine who worked with a television production crew, walked past. He saw my red eyes and the look on my face. "Dave," he called out. "Are you okay?" He noticed me rubbing the bracelet on my left wrist and asked me about it. I told him Jessy's story and what Lucas had said. I started to tear up again and, at that exact moment, we heard a noise overhead. We looked up as a large helicopter suddenly appeared, flying low just above the upper deck press box. It flew slowly over the field then stopped directly over home plate and hovered above us.

No flyover had been scheduled to take place. Bob pointed at the chopper and said, "Do you realize that is a Coast Guard Black Hawk? It has radar and sonar equipment instead of weapons." Otherwise, it was identical to the helicopter Jessy had been riding in when he was killed. I could hardly believe my eyes. After a moment, I took a deep breath. There was no doubt in my mind that that helicopter was a message from Jessy. The moment I came to that realization, the helicopter stopped hovering and slowly flew away over the field. I felt a great peace. Bob and I looked at each other with huge smiles. Not before or since have I ever seen another helicopter hover over the field like that.

I believe things happen for a reason, and I feel lucky to have had that experience. Even my PTSD happened for a reason. I know that now.

Chapter 1

$\mathcal{I}$ was probably the last kid in the world anyone would ever think might end up with PTSD. Of course, when I was growing up, no one even knew what PTSD was. It wasn't until 1980 that post-traumatic stress disorder became an official diagnosis. But who even thinks of things like that while growing up? All I cared about was baseball. It was a family tradition.

My grandfather, Big Bill Mellor, played for the Baltimore Orioles in the American League in 1902, the first year the American League was considered a major league. He went to Brown University in Providence, Rhode Island, then played semi-pro and minor league baseball before joining the Orioles for one season. After that, he shuffled between the minors and semi-pro before he returned to Brown as a coach. Eventually, he became a manager in the Blackstone Valley League, working at one of the mills and running the baseball team.

The Industrial Revolution began in the Blackstone River Valley. Huge textile mills lined the Blackstone River from Worcester, Massachusetts, to Providence and each employed thousands of people. A hundred years ago or so, the Blackstone Valley League, a big industrial semi-pro league, was one of the best semi-pro leagues in the country. The owners were very competitive and most of the mills sponsored baseball teams. They would play against each other after work and on weekends. The games drew thousands of people, often more than the Braves or Red Sox did in Boston. As a result, the mill owners recruited players from all over the country.

A lot of great ballplayers came from that area, like my grandfather's good friend, Hall-of-Famer Napoleon Lajoie, who was from Woonsocket, Rhode Island, and Gabby Hartnett from Millville, Massachusetts, who hit the famous "Homer in the Gloaming" that helped win the pennant for the Chicago Cubs in 1938. My grandfather managed a team in East Douglas, Massachusetts, for the Hayward-Schuster Woolen Mills.

Walter Schuster, who owned the mill, was exceptionally wealthy and paid his ballplayers well. In addition to their mill salaries, they would be paid extra to play ball. Some players, particularly pitchers, were paid a lot more, sometimes a couple of hundred dollars a game—big money in the 1920s and '30s. The newspapers nicknamed Schuster's team "the Millionaires." He occasionally even hired big league pitchers like Lefty Grove of the Philadelphia Athletics to pitch for Douglas in between big league starts, and Schuster was well enough connected that the Red Sox sometimes played exhibition games in Douglas, at Soldier's Field, on off days.

One team picture from the early 1930s shows my grandfather in uniform with his players. In the back row is Hank Greenberg, who later became a Hall of Fame first baseman for Detroit and Pittsburgh and is best known for being the first Jewish star in American sports. He was only nineteen when he played for my granddad, and I've been told he struggled. Yet, only two years later, he was in the majors.

My granddad was well known in the area. In 1939, the Red Sox celebrated an Old-Timer's Day. My grandfather was one of sixty-six players invited to attend, and our family still has the letter of invitation. It mentions some of his teammates that day: guys like Napoleon Lajoie, Ty Cobb, Babe Ruth, Walter Johnson, Honus Wagner. A who's who of all-stars and Hall of Famers...and my grandfather!

My Dad grew up in East Douglas and nearby in Rhode Island, and that's probably how he became a Red Sox fan—make that a Red Sox *fanatic*. That's kind of funny, really, because the Baltimore team my granddad played for moved to New York in 1903 and became the New York Yankees, Boston's arch rival. There are no Yankees fans in my family.

My Dad later became an executive for a woolen mill and met my mother, who is from South Carolina, while he was down there on a business trip. Before I was born, my family lived in several different cities in Massachusetts and New England. In fact, his company had two box seats right next to the visitor's dugout at Fenway Park. Unfortunately, I never had a chance to sit in them, but my older brother, Chip, attended several games with my Dad in those seats. They could hear the opposing manager talking to his players.

By the time I was born in 1963, we had moved to Piqua, Ohio, after my dad took a job with another company in the wool industry. I almost didn't make it. I was born with the umbilical cord wrapped around my chest and barely weighed three pounds. I wasn't breathing at birth and spent months in an incubator. My brothers weren't allowed in the room. They were introduced to me through a window. Although my parents worried that I might grow up disabled, I was very fortunate. I only ended up with baseball fever!

Three years later, the day before Mother's Day, 1966, my parents were out at a supper club in Dayton when my Dad started feeling dizzy and nauseous. He had previously had a couple of mild heart attacks, so my Mom got him to the hospital right away.

When she visited him the next day, he seemed to be doing okay. He was stable. They even listened to a baseball game together on the radio. She stayed until later that evening, told him good night, and drove home. When she walked in the door, the phone was ringing. My dad had died from a massive heart attack. He was only forty-eight years old.

I was three. If my father's death was traumatic for me at the time, I don't remember it. It was probably more difficult on the rest of my family. Chip was fifteen, Terry was ten, and our mother was suddenly a widow. She hadn't worked since having children, but she soon got a job with the local Presbyterian Church as an assistant to the pastor. She is an incredibly caring lady, always wanting to help people, the elderly, shut-ins, homeless, or anyone down on their luck. She has always been very giving, more worried about others than herself and working for the church was terrific for her. She and our family received a lot of support from the church and the community.

My mother worked so hard after my Dad died. We never had a great deal of money, but I don't remember ever really needing something and not having it. Somehow, she found a way, and she was always there to support and help me. She never thought of herself first. She thought of us.

Years later, *the New York Times* did a story on me and took my picture in the press box at Fenway, with the field in the background. After the story came out, Chip called and said "Hey, did you see anything interesting in that picture?"

I said, "No, why?"

He said "Well, the seats that are just over your shoulder are where Dad and I sat for the Red Sox games."

I walk by those seats ten to twenty times a day. Nearly every time I do now, I think of my brothers, and my mom and dad. It's almost like they are with me. For me, Fenway Park really does feel like home.

I only have one memory of my father, watching airplanes with him at a small local airport. I can see a long barn with propeller planes, a grass runway, and the windsock. I remember looking up and seeing my Dad. That's it.

Although there were times that not having a father made me feel different, that doesn't mean I had a bad childhood. Very quickly, my brothers went from being kids to being the men of the family. They became my Dad. Whenever there were father and son outings, they stepped in. And they did a great job. They taught me everything I needed to know about how to be a man, such as how to shave, how to treat others as you want to be treated, how to treat women with respect, and how to be both generous and humble. And, of course, they taught me how to play baseball.

We didn't have T-Ball in our town. You started out in Midget League, followed by Little League and Pony League before high school, then American Legion and Connie Mack baseball. Terry, who later played some baseball at Otterbein College, was my first coach in Midget League.

Mostly, I played wiffle ball in the backyard with some buddies and neighbors, Jim, John, and Jack—boys about my age. I would pretend to be the Red Sox and go to bat like Jim Rice, Dwight Evans, Carl Yastrzemski, or Fred Lynn, I knew the whole lineup. I'd also pretend to pitch like Luis Tiant, spinning all the way around and turning my back to the batter. We would play for hours, until it was dark, and the only light left came from the lightning bugs. Then, late that night, I would often call the local radio station, deepening my voice so they would think I was an adult, and ask for the Red Sox score. I don't know if I fooled them, but I usually found out the score.

We had a fence in our backyard that was six feet high. Naturally, we nicknamed it "the Green Monster." Anything over that was a home run. A maple tree was the foul pole down the left field line, and three arborvitae shrubs made the right field line. Any ball that bounced to the fence was a single. Base runners were ghost men we kept track of as they ran base to base. If the ball hit the fence on the fly or got stuck in a tree, it was a double. We'd throw the bat at it to get it down and sometimes the bat would get stuck. That was about the only thing that ever kept us from playing!

When we got a little older, we graduated from my backyard, which wasn't very big, to our neighbor's yard, two houses down. Actually, we combined two yards; one was mostly the infield, while the other was the outfield.

We played so much we wore bare spots in the grass where the pitcher and batter stood. I often think about that now, because our neighbor, an older man, never complained about that. He couldn't have been nicer. Every time I see kids playing in a yard somewhere or see the happiness on a kid's face when he or she has the opportunity to be on the field at Fenway, I think of him. I hope he realized just how much joy he gave us.

It's funny now, after all that damage we did to his backyard, that I'm responsible for keeping the field at Fenway looking good. It's funny, too, to think that, when I was growing up, in addition to teaching me how to play baseball, my brothers taught me how to take care of the lawn and cut the grass. It's almost like they knew what I would end up doing for a living.

Although I worked at a grocery store while in high school, I usually made money mowing lawns. Terry showed me how. I wanted to make sure I did it right, so that, if my brothers ever checked on me, I would make them proud. That meant mowing wheel on wheel, where each wheel mark on each pass precisely overlaps the previous one, and mowing in lines as straight as laser beams, all with a push mower. They made sure that, whatever I did, whether edging or trimming, that I did it right. They taught me that it wasn't ethical to take someone's money if you didn't give a full days' work, or if you didn't do what you were supposed to do. From the start, they taught me to pay attention to detail and take pride in what I did, whether that was cutting grass, playing ball, or anything else. Although I missed my father growing up, a lot of kids with fathers never had the great experience I had being raised by my brothers. Whenever I needed them, they were there.

Of course, there were times I missed my dad, and holidays were always sort of awkward. There would sometimes be functions and somebody from our church would fill in, maybe at a father-son picnic, in a one-legged race or something, and it was always kind of uncomfortable. I'd see my buddies doing stuff with their fathers, and I'm sure there were times my brothers tried to help me, and I'd say something mean like, "You're my brother, not my dad."

I may have learned to hide my feelings, but it also made me stronger, more self-reliant, and to appreciate family more. I'd sometimes hear my friends complain, "Hey, my Dad grounded me. I hate him."

I would try to explain to them, "You don't mean that. You don't understand what it's like to not have a dad."

Every year, my brothers would take me to Riverfront Stadium in Cincinnati to see a couple of Reds games. There was a little drugstore in our hometown that sold tickets and my mom would let me go through the schedule at the start of the season. Back then, there were a lot of special promotions and doubleheaders, and I'd try to pick a doubleheader that was a bat day or helmet day, so I could not only see a couple games, but come home with a souvenir.

In 1972, Terry took me down to see a World Series game when the Reds played the A's. But in 1975, the Red Sox made the World

Series and we went to all three games in Cincinnati. No way were we going to miss that. Almost everybody else in the area was a Reds fan, but we were rooting for the Sox. We weren't shy about it either.

Riverfront Stadium was nothing like Fenway Park. It was just a big round concrete bowl with artificial turf. In the upper deck, the stands were so steep that it made you feel as though, if you fell, you'd just roll right down the aisle and onto the field.

I didn't care where the seats were. I was just thrilled to be there, even way up high, about ten rows from the front of the upper deck. Before we went, we decided to make a banner to support the Red Sox. We took a bed sheet, spread it out in the basement, and painted "GO RED SOX" and "GO BOSTON" on it along with the names of the players: Yaz, El Tiante, Fred Lynn, Jim Rice, and the others.

We spent hours making it perfect. We planned to parade it around the park before hanging it from the facade of the upper deck, so EVERYONE would see it.

This took planning. By this time, Chip was away at school, so it was up to Terry to come up with the plan. And he did, paying attention to every detail. He folded up the banner and hid it under his coat. He took a bamboo fishing pole, the kind that screwed together in segments, and stuck it down his pant legs. We planned to put the banner on the poles once we got inside but, first, we had to sneak the poles in. I remember as he walked he looked like the Tin Man before Dorothy loosened up his joints.

It worked! We made it inside. But when we got to the upper deck and Terry took the poles out of his pants, this lady—I think she was an usher—saw them and took them from us. We shifted to Plan B. Our seats were in about the tenth row. We went down to the front row of the upper deck, unfurled our banner and tied it to the rail. I was so excited and proud. I thought, "Wow, maybe we'll get on TV!"

Of course, Reds fans didn't appreciate seeing a banner supporting the Red Sox. We went back to our seats and heard this lady screaming obscenities at us while trying to untie our banner. We raced down to get it and she kept screaming at us as we walked it back to our seats. I couldn't believe how worked up she got! Eventually, we just hung the sign on the back wall of the upper deck. That didn't get much of a better reaction. Reds fans poured beer on it and gave us a hard time all game long.

That was bad enough, but I was absolutely crushed when the Sox lost the series in seven games. It broke my heart, like it did to so many other Sox fans. At the same time, it made me love them even more. If rooting for the Sox taught you anything, it was how to live with heartbreak and how to be patient. I always looked forward to next year.

At the same time, baseball was becoming more serious to me. When you play wiffle ball, you mostly just pitch and hit. When I started playing hardball, I largely played outfield, only pitching once in a while. I played in a summer league in junior high and, when I reached Piqua High, our team already had a bunch of seniors playing outfield. I knew my chances of making the varsity team weren't very good. I went to the coach and asked, "What is the quickest way I can get to varsity and be a regular player?"

"Do you know how to pitch?" he asked?

I knew how to *throw*, so I said I was pitcher. Now I had to learn to do what I said could.

I was pretty good-sized, close to six feet tall, and all I knew then about pitching was to throw as hard as I could for as long as I could. I never thought about placing the ball or changing speeds and, while I was growing up, Terry wouldn't let me throw a curve, as he was trying to protect my arm. Now that I was a pitcher, though, I figured I had to start throwing one, so I did, over and over and over again.

Of course, I wasn't throwing it very well, and I certainly wasn't throwing it the right way. My elbow got sore. I literally couldn't lift my arm to comb my hair. I even went to a chiropractor to try to get some relief, but I was too afraid to tell our coach. If I did, I was afraid that he might not let me play, so I just sucked it up and tried to do my best.

That's how we approached things in my family. You didn't complain. Complaining was a sign of weakness. You sucked it up and kept going. While that may work in a lot of situations, I realize now how that attitude may have led to me bottling things up instead of letting others know what's going on. But, when you're a teenager, you don't know any better. Sometimes you don't learn how important it can be to express your feelings until keeping everything inside causes problems. That's something my experience with PTSD has taught me: we never stop learning and growing, and it is never too late to change or ask for help. The beginning of a solution to a problem is never far away. All you have to do is ask. That's not weakness. That's the strength of knowing that you have to face your problems.

I think about that often. It's one of the primary reasons I decided to write this book—so others could learn from my story. PTSD doesn't just affect you, it affects everyone around you. Getting treatment can be as much for them as it is for you. Later, you may realize, as I did, that it is something you should have done long before.

For years, I treated my PTSD the way I treated that sore arm: I ignored it, hoping it would go away. But, while my sore arm did get better, the pain from PTSD lingered much longer.

The summer after my sophomore year, I finally started to figure out what I was doing on the mound. My control improved, and I had a really good year. That continued into the next season. My junior year, we entered the state Legion baseball tournament as the number one team in our class, and we made it all the way to the semifinals. Tim Belcher pitched and led his team to an eleven-inning 1-0 win. He later ended up going to Mount Vernon Nazarene College before being drafted. At the time, there were two drafts of amateur players each year and, in 1983, Belcher was the number one pick in both, first by the Twins and, when he didn't sign, by the Yankees.

The following summer, I played on both a travel team and the local American Legion team. Both teams went to the state tournament and our Legion team made the semi-finals. I think I went 11-0 or something. I was still just throwing hard, but then my coach taught me how to throw a changeup. I'll never forget being at the state tournament in Athens, Ohio, striking out four straight guys in one inning after my catcher missed a third strike, and getting the last guy on three straight changeups. I couldn't believe that it was possible to throw more slowly and get more strikeouts. That should have taught me something but, most of the time, I still just tried to throw the ball as hard as I could. I thought that was the path to a college scholarship and then the big leagues. I was beginning to realize I might have the opportunity to do that. Baseball scouts and college coaches were starting to take a closer look at me. My dream of playing baseball in the major leagues seemed possible.

It wasn't the way it is now, where top players are scouted years in advance, are ranked by internet recruiters, and often select their colleges in their junior year. When I was in high school, many baseball players didn't decide where to go to college until after their final season. A lot of colleges waited until then to make scholarship offers.

Early in my senior year, our coach pulled the whole team together before one game. He yelled, "David, there are head coaches from some colleges in the stands, so don't fuck up." He was trying to pump me up. And he did. WAY up. I tried to throw the ball through my catcher, through the umpire, through the backstop and through the bleachers. Ball one, ball two, ball three, and take your base. I walked the bases loaded on something like fourteen pitches. After the third walk, I saw one of the college coaches get up and leave. I remember thinking: "Oh, no. What did I just do?" Then I turned it around. I think I struck out the next three guys on nine pitches. The game went ten innings. I pitched the whole thing and we eventually won but, at the time, I thought I may have blown my chance for a scholarship.

I hadn't. I had another good year, and, by the end of the season, I was being contacted by some Division 1 schools with really good reputations like Southern Illinois, which, under legendary coach Itch Jones, went to the College World Series almost every year, the University of Toledo, Ohio University, which is where Mike Schmidt played, and Ohio State, which was a real powerhouse. My coach encouraged me to take my time before deciding on a school, even after the high school season ended. I was playing for American Legion Post 184. We were really good and entered the state Connie Mack tournament as one of the favorites. The colleges were certain to pay attention. I wasn't the only player they were interested in either. Our catcher, Mike Day, was literally the best ball player I played with, as well as the nicest guy in the world. He ended up at Oklahoma State where he was a four-year starter and got drafted by the Expos. He caught Randy Johnson in the minors. Unfortunately, he broke his arm in the same place twice and had to quit after only a few seasons.

I knew a lot of colleges would be scouting the tournament. My coach said, "Look, you've got a few colleges interested in you. Go and pitch well there and you're gonna have more offers and more people interested. If I were you, I would wait, before you sign anything." I saw no reason not to wait, so I did.

I was also being looked at by pro scouts. At least, they knew who I was. At one point, I was invited to attend a tryout camp held by the Reds in Piqua. Only about thirty players were invited, and I was one of only four or five pitchers. Of course, Tim Belcher, who was in college by now, was there, and almost everybody else was a great ballplayer and athlete. It was a real eye opener. At the start of the tryout, everyone, even pitchers, had to run the sixty-yard dash. I was slow. On my left was Keith Byars, an All-State in both football and basketball, who ended up being a star running back at Ohio State and later played in the NFL. On my right was a Latino ballplayer who I think had recently escaped from Cuba. The race started and, honest to God, I think they were both across the finish line before I was even halfway. Good thing I was a pitcher. You don't have to run fast to pitch.

Then I went down by the bullpen with the other pitchers. We warmed up and Tim Belcher was the first to take the mound. A scout timed every pitch with a radar gun. Belcher was just so fluid. It looked like he was just playing catch. Tim threw one pitch—*one pitch*—and they told him, "Tim, that's great, super. Just go sit in the dugout and we'll talk to you in a few minutes." I think that one pitch was clocked at ninety-three miles an hour or something, faster than a lot of guys were throwing in the majors then, and the fastest pitch I had ever seen up close.

I was no Tim Belcher. I knew that. But his coach at Mount Nazarene College had talked to me about maybe going there and had told me I would be their number-two starter as a freshman. At some other colleges, I knew I would have to bide my time behind upper classmen.

I took the mound and threw about a dozen pitches. The fastest might have been eighty-seven miles per hour. Good for a high school pitcher and intriguing enough for college coaches, but hardly enough to get drafted out of high school. The scout stopped me and said, "David, thanks for coming. You're done for the day." That was it. My tryout was done. I'd given my heart and soul to the game, but I realized I wasn't ready yet. I knew I needed to go to college and get better to try to make it to the major leagues.

Years later, when Tim was pitching coach for the Indians, I met him and mentioned the tryout. He didn't remember it, and I don't think he remembered me, but he couldn't have been nicer.

Baseball was still all I was thinking about. I didn't party in high school or go on a lot of dates. I did okay in school and I had a vague notion of studying business in college, although I had no idea what that meant. I wanted to pitch, to play ball, to make baseball my life. There was no Plan B. Everything seemed to be falling into place. I had just graduated from high school and the state Connie Mack tournament was coming up in late July. I looked forward to pitching and then deciding on a college. After that, I hoped to get stronger, throw harder, pitch better, and get drafted by a big-league team—hopefully the Red Sox!—and follow my grandfather to the majors.

That was my dream. But on July 10, 1981, that dream turned into twenty-nine years of nightmares.

Chapter 2

*D*o you know the old saying "Red sky in the morning, sailors take warning. Red sky at night, sailor's delight"? Well, the sunset that evening was incredible. I watched it for a minute and thought, "That's good stuff." School was out, I was working at the grocery store, playing ball, and looking forward to college. I'm incredibly superstitious and that sunset seemed like a pretty good omen.

It was a Saturday. Earlier that day, my buddy Jim White, who lived up the street, called to ask if I wanted to do something. I said sure, so we went for a bike ride around our little town, not really going anywhere, just waiting for the rest of our lives to begin.

It was a warm, muggy day. At one point, we were on a busy road, one of the few in town that was four lanes across. Jim was ahead of me. The light was green and, just as I entered the intersection, the light turned yellow. Out of nowhere, I heard this car coming. It had run the red light. It missed me, but it was so close I could feel the breeze as the car shot by. That scared the heck out of me and, after I got through the intersection, I pulled over. Jim, having seen it all, circled back.

"Oh, man," he said, "this is your lucky day. That thing almost hit you."

I caught my breath and we soon started joking about it. We rode around for a while more and I eventually went back home. I thought Jim was right. I was lucky. Everything in my life was going great.

Later that day, one of my teammates called to ask if I wanted to see "Stripes," a Bill Murray movie about being in the Army. It was a big hit then and the trailer on TV was hilarious. I said sure. We went to a show early that evening. I was wearing a brand-new pair of blue jeans and a watch I had gotten for graduation. I picked him up in my mom's Ford LTD and we drove to the theater in Troy, Ohio, just fifteen miles up the freeway. It was a funny movie and I enjoyed it.

We hopped back into the car and as we were leaving my buddy said, "Hey, do you want to stop and get something to eat?"

"Sure," I said. As we drove off, I saw that sunset.

There was a McDonald's just before the freeway, so we decided to go there. My absolute favorite thing was to get French fries and a milkshake. It sounds gross, but I just loved dipping the fries in the milkshake. I don't think I had ever been to that McDonald's before and wasn't familiar with it, but I pulled in and parked on the right side of the lot, sort of opposite the entrance, which was on the side. We both got out and started walking across the lot to the door.

"Oh, man," I said, "I forgot my wallet. I left it in the car."

"All right," he said. "I'm gonna go on in."

I returned to the car, got my wallet, closed the door and took a few steps back toward the restaurant. Right then, I noticed this car pull in abruptly from the street. The car was only fifty or sixty feet away, and the way it had screeched to a stop startled me. It was dusk, and the streetlights were on. Some cars had their headlights on, but there was plenty of light left. I remember the car was dark and big. I stood there watching as the driver and passenger, both women, each got out of the car and switched sides, a younger woman getting into the passenger's seat and a woman a few years older, maybe in her thirties, a little heavy set, moving to the driver's seat. I later found out that the younger woman was an inexperienced driver and was worried about steering the car through the drive-through. That was why they stopped and switched. I motioned with my arm for them to go ahead. Then they waved for me to go, so I started walking across the lot toward the door.

I remember well the sound of the engine revving, the tires squealing. I turned to see the car barreling straight at me.

"What the hell are they doing?"

There was no time to run. I could only turn, raise my hand and lift my left leg, kind of like a flamingo, trying to get as much of my body out of the way as possible. The next thing I knew I was in the air and flying toward the red brick wall of the McDonald's. The entranceway jutted out. I flew past it and crumpled into a pile in the corner, my head striking the bricks. I could still hear the car. I lifted my head to see it was still coming, racing toward me. I was going to be hit again!

There was a black steel handrail leading up to the door. When the car's chrome bumper struck it, I heard the horrible shriek of metal striking metal and saw sparks filling the air. Landing where I had protected me a little. Otherwise, the car would have hit me flush. It couldn't quite reach me. But, in that instant, the handrail folded over and the car struck me a second time, the rail and the bumper pinning my right knee against the wall. Glass broke around me and fragments of bricks showered down on me. I couldn't move.

The engine was still revving, the tires still spinning as the car pressed up against me. I felt the heat from the engine. The smoke and exhaust choked me. I could see her over the hood, behind the steering wheel, just sitting there, staring at me, frozen. I started screaming and yelling, pleading, "Turn off the car! Turn off the car! Turn off the car!"

Only then did I feel the pain. My heart beat in my throat, my body ached, and my knee throbbed, but it was like time had stopped. I looked over my shoulder into the window of the McDonald's. It was cracked and there were faces pressed up against the glass, just staring at me while I was screaming, like I was an animal in the zoo. There was a door only a few feet away to my left and I couldn't understand why somebody hadn't come out to help.

Everything moved in slow motion. I could see my friend on the other side of the glass. He appeared to be talking to me, but I couldn't understand him. My ears were ringing, my head throbbing, the engine roaring.... His mouth was moving, but I couldn't understand what he was saying. I kept screaming and yelling and begging for someone to turn off the engine, so the car would back off. Nobody did anything. No one came to help. It seemed like I was there forever, just screaming my lungs out.

Someone inside must have called the police. After three or four minutes, I noticed the flashing lights of a police car. Then a light burst in my face as someone moved around the car. It was a newspaper photographer. Instead of helping, he was taking pictures while I lay pinned to the building.

My mind was racing. I started to worry. Someone had to call my Mom—my brothers had moved away, and she was all alone. I was supposed to pitch in the Connie Mack tournament. *"Am I going to be able to play?"*

Finally, an officer arrived. He must have pulled the woman out the car, gotten in, put the car in reverse, and backed away. The instant the pressure was released from my knee a wave of incredible pain shot through my leg and out into my body. I felt like passing out. I had a massive headache, but I wasn't bleeding—at least, not that I could tell. I started shaking uncontrollably and broke out into a cold sweat.

The officer came to my side and tried to reassure me, telling me that an ambulance was on its way and to keep calm and still. Then the EMTs showed up, took my vital signs, and lifted me onto a gurney. I was in pain like I had never been in pain before but, more than that, I was worried. Somebody had to call my mom and tell her. I didn't want her to worry.

The medics started cutting off my jeans because my right knee was already so swollen they couldn't get my pants down. I was crushed. I had gotten the jeans for graduation and it wasn't like we could afford new jeans every week. Now I was worried about that. The watch I had gotten for graduation was damaged too. The crystal was scratched.

By now, my friend was out of the restaurant and trying to talk to me, but my ears were still ringing, and I couldn't understand him. I was furious at the woman who hit me. I couldn't understand how she could have done what she did. I hated her. I felt like she screwed my life over. As it turned out, she wasn't drunk or impaired or anything. She just stepped on the accelerator instead of the brake and panicked. That's it. It was just a mistake—a stupid, simple accident. But one that changed my life forever.

I barely remember the ride to the hospital. The siren was loud, my head was pounding, and I was in a panic, a thousand thoughts running through my head, worrying about everything—my Mom, the tournament, college, everything. I didn't know what was happening. All of a sudden, my entire future was uncertain.

As I was wheeled into the emergency room, doctors and nurses swarmed all over me, ordering X-rays and tests and poking and prodding me, shining lights in my eyes, asking me if this or that hurt, then talking to each other in medical shorthand that I couldn't begin to understand.

I just wanted to know what was wrong, how badly I was hurt, but they wouldn't tell me anything. They said they needed to wait until my mother arrived. It was only a ten or fifteen-minute drive, and I knew she must be really worried after getting the call and not knowing how badly I was hurt. Every thought I had created more anxiety.

I had never been badly injured before. The previous summer, I had gone rafting in the Grand Canyon with my bother Chip and had been stung on the face by a scorpion, and I broke my wrist once sledding, but neither of those came close to this. The nurses, the doctors, even the orderlies, were all being vague, which only made me worry more. I was thinking: *Is something seriously wrong? Is that why they won't tell me anything?*

They did X-rays of my head and knees and then my mother arrived. I was so relieved to see her. She came over and held my hand and told me everything was going to be all right. I didn't know if that was true or not, but it sure felt good to hear her say it.

We were still in the emergency room, my bed curtained off, when a doctor finally came in. He told us that I may have a concussion but that, according to the X-rays, I didn't have any broken bones. But there was something wrong with my knee. It was significantly swollen, but he said whatever it was wouldn't show up on the X-ray. There were no MRI machines or anything like that then. He told us I would have to see a knee specialist to talk about my ligaments. I had no idea what that meant, but I knew it wasn't good. He gave us the name of a doctor in Dayton. They didn't even admit me to the hospital. They told my mom to take me home, have me lie down, and stay quiet and call the specialist as soon as possible. Before I left, they put my knee in an immobilizer and wrapped it an ice pack with a big ace bandage. Then they gave us a set of crutches and told my mom to ice it off and on all night. I can't remember if they gave me anything for the pain, but I got up and was still feeling sore. I went out to the car feeling unsteady on my crutches and somehow managed to get in before we drove home.

Nobody had said anything about not playing baseball, and I was still worried about that. But until someone said I couldn't play, I was still planning to pitch in the tournament.

When we got home, I started to realize that probably wouldn't happen. To get in the house, I had to climb three stairs. My mom went first and held the doors open, but I could barely get up the stairs; I was worried I was going to tumble backwards.

I went straight to bed. My mom arranged pillows under my knee to support my leg, then got another ice bag and put it on my knee. I lay back. My entire body was still throbbing. I lay awake for a long time, replaying the accident in my head and worrying about my future before finally falling asleep. Maybe it would all be better in the morning.

I had a nightmare that I was wide awake, my heart racing, and all I could see was the car in front of me. I could hear the engine and smell the exhaust. Everything came flooding back as if it was still happening. I must have screamed, because suddenly my mother was in the room standing next to me, telling me it was okay, that I was all right, and that I was home.

I realize now that that was the first sign of PTSD. I had a nightmare the next night too, and the one after that, and the one after that, sometimes as many as four or five a night. I would have at least one nightmare every single night of my life for the next twenty-nine years. Tens of thousands of nightmares.

I didn't know about PTSD. I doubt I had even heard of it before. The term was just coming into use by doctors, who were trying to find a way to describe the symptoms of veterans returning from Vietnam who experienced flashbacks.

Today we understand that PTSD can be caused by all sorts of trauma, from warfare to assault, from sexual abuse to being in a car accident. PTSD is not just a condition that affects veterans. I went nearly three decades before I made the connection between my symptoms and PTSD.

In all that time, PTSD was never mentioned to me. Over time, as my nightmares increased, and other symptoms became more acute, I was ashamed. I thought I was messed up inside, that there was something mentally or emotionally wrong with me, and it became almost a full-time job to keep anyone from finding out just how messed up I was on the inside.

When I woke up the next morning, I realized what had happened the night before was no dream. You know the expression that you feel like you "got run over by a truck"? Well, that's exactly how I felt. Everything ached, all my muscles, my head was still hurting, and my knee was really sore. It was still swollen. I thought it would be all black and blue, but it wasn't. It was just red and sore.

My mother called the specialist on Monday and we got an appointment right away. Dayton was only thirty-five miles away, but the drive seemed to take forever. I was still very uncomfortable and concerned.

The doctor's office was sterile and old-fashioned. I remember sitting in the waiting room and everybody there was on crutches and had casts on. I was still wearing the immobilizer. They called my name and I went into the exam room. They got me up on a table and the doctor started manipulating my knee, bending it back and forth and side to side. When he bent it to the inside, it hurt so badly that I thought it was going to break, like a chicken wing. I actually screamed out.

He said he thought there might be a meniscus tear. Then he had to check the medial collateral ligament, which is the one that runs in the inside part of your knee and keeps it from bending inward.

"Uh-huh. Well, we'll have to do surgery," he said.

I was shocked. I couldn't believe it. I guess I was still hoping it was just a bad bruise.

"Can I play baseball again?" I asked. That was all I cared about. If passion alone could get you into the majors, then I would've made it.

The doctor paused. "I won't be sure till I get in there," he said. "I think I can fix it, hopefully, with an arthroscope. And, if that's the case, you should be able to play again."

That was a big relief. Arthroscopic surgery, where they make only a small incision, was still relatively brand new, but I knew that was much better than the old kind of surgery, which was much more invasive and took much longer to recover from. I knew the Connie Mack tournament was out, but all I heard was, "You should be able to play again."

The next week went by quickly. I was still having nightmares every night, but I didn't yet realize how serious that was. I just wanted to get the surgery over and start rehabilitation. I knew that college baseball teams started working out late in the fall, and I hoped to be ready for that.

After the surgery, I expected to wake up to see my knee in an immobilizer and an ace bandage. With arthroscopic surgery, there's usually no need for a cast. I thought I'd start rehabbing and working out in a few weeks. It would be difficult, and I would have to work as hard as I could, progressing slowly, one base at a time, but I would come back and pitch again and make it to the majors. I had no doubt about that. But, as I came out of anesthesia, I was in a lot of pain. I reached for my knee. I felt this thing on my leg that wasn't supposed to be there, and it shook me out of my daze. I opened my eyes and looked down. There was a cast on my leg that ran from my ankle to my hip. The plaster was still warm.

This was much more serious than I had imagined.

Chapter 3

*W*hen I left the hospital, I knew my knee was damaged and crushed, but I did not realize that my dream of making it to the majors had also been destroyed. I had a lot of bitterness inside toward the woman who hit me and even toward myself. I held that hatred inside a long time.

Knowing what I know now, however, the day that I was hit was one of the luckiest days of my life. If that had never happened, I would never have met my wife, Denise, and never would have had my two girls. Maybe I would have played college baseball, maybe even made the majors, but I wouldn't have what I have now. But, as I looked down at my leg in the cast, I wasn't thinking that then. I was only thinking of what I had lost.

I was in the cast for close to two months, and there wasn't much more I could do but lie in bed and watch television. I went to see my team play ball, but I didn't really feel like I was part of it anymore. I was in a great deal of pain, so, apart from occasional physical therapy to maintain some strength in my leg, I mostly stayed home.

Baseball was out, but I was still confident that, once the cast came off, I would pitch in college. The University of Toledo started a little later than many other schools, their coach was still interested in me, and some friends of mine were going there, so, at the end of the summer, I enrolled.

It was great to finally feel like I was moving forward again with my life. I remember that, when my cast finally came off, I couldn't even bend my knee. The whole leg had atrophied so much that it was barely bigger around than my arm. And the smell! All my friends had signed my cast and I had thought it might be kind of neat to keep it but, as soon as they took it off, about two months of sweat stunk up the room. I couldn't throw it away fast enough.

My leg was weak, so I had to wear an immobilizer and walk on crutches, but at least I could move again. I even figured out how to drive. I couldn't bend or lift my leg to get in on the driver's side door, but I could pull myself out that way. Fortunately, my car, the "Green Meanie," had a single bench seat in front. To get in, I had to slide onto the passenger's seat and pull myself over to the driver's side, then use my left foot on the gas and brake. I tied a jump rope to the passenger's door so, once I was in, I could pull it closed.

After spending most of the summer feeling sorry for myself, it was exciting to finally go away to college. Naturally, I was nervous too, not only about being on my own, but because I was still having nightmares. I worried that, if I had them at school and woke up my roommate, he might think I was weird or something. Wearing the brace already made me feel different enough.

I ended up rooming with one of my friends from Piqua. I took the bottom bunk. We shared the dorm with a bunch of members of the football team, just opposite the baseball field. Every day, I looked out at the field and saw myself pitching the following spring.

Those first few weeks were a lot of fun. Even though I was still on crutches I tried to do everything everyone else was doing. I ended up with blisters the size of silver dollars on my palms and my armpits were rubbed raw.

My roommate was an incredible guy. Although I was still having nightmares, I never talked to him about them, so, every night before I went to sleep, I was scared that he'd hear me. Back home, I had stopped having friends over for sleepovers because I was afraid they might hear me. Now I was anxious about going to sleep, so I'd watch TV until I nodded off, hoping that, if I did yell out, the sound would drown out my screams or I could blame it on the TV. My roommate never said a word about any of it. I had a hard time getting around on crutches and he helped carry my books and get me through doorways. He couldn't have been more considerate.

I was having flashbacks, although I didn't yet have a name for what I was experiencing. I just thought I was messed up. All I knew was that certain things caused a negative reaction I could not control—tires squealing, an engine revving, the smell of McDonald's French fries. Any of these caused the hair on the back of my neck to stand up. I'd start sweating profusely, my heart pounded, and my chest tightened. It almost hurt to breathe deeply. Sometimes I got headaches. After these attacks, I'd look around wondering if anybody had noticed and was staring at me.

Although I now view the flashbacks as a sign of strength and proof that I'm a survivor, I didn't look at them that way then. I felt like jumping out of my skin and, if I had one around other people, I tried to make it seem like I was making some kind of joke. Almost every waking hour, I worried about that and found myself avoiding places that might trigger a flashback. It didn't leave me with much to do.

At the same time, I was starting physical therapy. I had to start slow, with basic range-of-motion movements, leg extensions, and hamstring curls to work on my flexibility. I gradually transitioned to using machines and lifting light weights. I realized this was going to take a long time, but I was determined to do whatever the therapists said to get better. My goal was to make the majors.

About five or six weeks into my first semester, I was sitting in our room with my immobilizer off, letting it air out, my leg on the desk, just looking out the window, when I heard my roommate coming down the hall. I stood up on my crutches as he came in, but I didn't put the immobilizer back on. He had a towel in his hands. He saw me standing there and as he entered the room he said, "Take a bow. The King's in town." Horsing around, he snapped the towel at my groin. I laughed and reacted without thinking, trying to block the towel with my hands while turning to avoid being hit. It was the simplest little thing. For a split second I forgot all about my knee. As I turned, I lost my balance and my crutches went out from under me. For the first time since my accident, I put my full weight on my bad leg without wearing the brace. My knee wasn't strong enough to support me. It buckled inward and sent a sharp pain through leg. I knew right away something was wrong. My buddy knew it too and began apologizing, but I didn't want to make him feel bad. I tried to laugh it off, to act like it was no big deal, but I knew that it was. A short time later, I called my Mom and she made an appointment for me to see my doctor in Dayton the next day.

I lay on the table while the doctor manipulated my leg, first the left one, for comparison, and then the right. It bent in far more than it should have, and the pain was incredible. The medial collateral ligament, which had been damaged in the accident, had torn. I would need more surgery and several more months in a cast. It did not seem possible. Just like that, I was back where I had started. The very next day we had to go back up to Toledo to withdraw from school. We went back to the dorm and packed everything we had unpacked just a few weeks before, and I had to leave all the friends I had just started to make. As I drove off with my mother, I remember looking at the baseball field, out to the pitcher's mound, wondering when I would be coming back. I tried to look at it as a setback, but it was hard not to feel disappointed. I also felt horrible for my roommate, because he was such a good guy and had helped me in so many ways. I hoped to return for the spring semester, but that depended on my leg.

There was no talk of arthroscopic surgery this time, even though we found a surgeon who was a little more sports-oriented—he was the surgeon for several university football teams. We hoped that, because he was involved in sports medicine, the outcome might be a little better.

The surgery took place about a week later, this time made a little more difficult because the scar tissue that had built up had to be removed. The surgeon had to open my entire knee and redo the surgery I had done in July. Once again, I woke with a cast from my ankle to my groin. At least this time I wasn't surprised.

I was fitted with a harness to help me get around in the cast. A padded strap went over my right shoulder and a belt around my waist. Two straps plastered to the top front of my cast were then fastened to the harness. That way, when I raised my shoulder the cast would lift up. It made it easier to use the crutches, but it was embarrassing—I looked like I was wearing my patrol uniform from sixth grade.

For the next few months, I had a brace again and was hyper-aware of my knee, worried that I was going to fall. I was ultra-careful, so nothing would happen, because I still wanted to pitch. Between my worries over the nightmares, the flashbacks, and my knee, I was almost paranoid. Every day, I was getting better at keeping my feelings and my fears hidden. I realize now how much energy that took, and how it caused me to miss out on so many things, not just then, but for most of the next three decades.

That's what is so insidious about PTSD. It changes the way you relate to the world and affects every relationship you have. For years, I just kept hoping my symptoms would go away, that, one day, I would wake up and be "normal" again. I never did.

After the cast came off, the doctor gave me some simple non-weight-bearing exercises to do to get ready to start physical therapy, and I did everything he told me to do. Just before Christmas, he gave me the "Okay" and handed me a prescription to begin supervised physical therapy at the hospital. I couldn't wait. My knee was no worse off than before my first surgery. I was ready to start healing and getting better.

The doctor warned me to be smart. He knew how eager I was to get back on the field. He told me to start with low weights, like five pounds, and that, if everything went well, we'd gradually increase the weight each week by a two and half pounds. He didn't want the therapist to be too aggressive. I remember that I was assigned to the head therapist and I was excited about that. I looked up to him just like I did a doctor. I figured he had to be the best possible person for me to work with and I promised myself to do everything he said.

I went in for the first time on a Monday and met my therapist. He was older—about forty, and balding. He wore a white coat, just like a doctor, and, in my mind, he was just as knowledgeable. The PT department didn't look anything like they do now, usually bright and airy with all sorts of specialized equipment. This was cold and sterile, a series of small rooms with a single table in each, not very welcoming. It wasn't nearly as advanced as the physical therapy department at the University. There, they had things like Cybex machines that allowed you to control your range of motion. I took off my brace and sat on the side of a padded therapy table. It was amazing how atrophied my leg was. I could put my hands around my thighs and touch my fingers and thumbs. All the muscle seemed to be gone. The skin was flabby and just hung there, like an old ladies' arm. I basically hadn't used it for almost six months. I hadn't even done anything yet and I was already embarrassed.

Somehow, the physical therapist knew I played baseball.

"Do you want to play baseball again?" he asked.

"Absolutely, yes, sir," I said. "It's my dream."

"Well, you need to do everything I say, and you got to work hard."

I said, "Okay." He was the doctor, after all; or he was in my mind, at least.

I sat on the edge of a treatment table with my legs hanging over the side. The therapist took a tube sock partially filled with sand, strapped it around my ankle with an ACE bandage and asked me to straighten out my leg. I was kind of surprised by that. I expected them to have a more professional setup, with real ankle weights like I'd seen in Toledo. But what did I know? I tried to straighten my leg. At first it barely moved. Then I slowly lifted it out, and then back down. Then I did it again. And again. It took absolutely everything I had. I couldn't believe how my leg was quivering. The side of my knee throbbed. I was exhausted and sweating like I had just pitched a complete game. I felt as weak as a baby. My thighs had been the strongest part of my body. In high school I could lift all the plates on the universal machine and did more leg extensions than the friends I worked out with. Everybody knows a pitcher gets power from his legs, and now my right leg was barely working.

I was supposed to do a full set, twelve lifts or something. I couldn't come close to that. I was mad that I couldn't do more, and I thought to myself, "This is going to be a much longer road than I thought." I did a few more exercises, but they weren't any easier. When I finished, the therapist put some ice on my knee and said, "Come back Wednesday."

On Wednesday, two days later, I remember him pushing on the inside of my knee and cracking some joke, like it was funny. Once again, he told me I had to work harder, that if I really wanted to get better, "we have to get aggressive and you really have to listen to me." If the guy had told me to jump off the roof, I probably would have done it. This time, he took three five-pound tube socks and ACE-bandaged them on to my ankle—three times as much weight as on Monday, which was already twice as much as the doctor had said. "And," I thought to myself, "that's a lot more weight than the doctor talked about. If I couldn't do the lesser weight a couple days earlier, how am I going to do this?" I couldn't even straighten my leg. I gripped the edge of the table and tried so hard my whole body was just trembling, my leg shaking. No matter what, I just could not raise my leg. It was an incredible blow emotionally and psychologically. I remember wondering, "If I couldn't do it Monday and I can't do it today, where do I go from here?" I felt like a total failure. In my mind, I was starting to question the therapist, but who was I? What did I know? I told myself, "I just have to do what he says so I can play baseball again."

When we were finished, he took off the ACE bandage and the weight, put some ice on my knee, and told me to come back Friday and "be ready to work harder."

On Friday, he asked me how it was going, and I told him my knee was still pretty sore from Wednesday. He said, "Well, do you want to play baseball again?"

I said "Yes, sir!" He might as well have asked me if I wanted to breathe.

He almost sounded angry. He was abrupt with me, like he was pissed off. Once again, he told me I had to "work harder. You gotta fight." I don't know if he was mad or just impatient or if that was just the way he tried to motivate people. I was already prepared to run through a wall to play baseball again. I don't think I needed any special motivation.

He had me sit on the side of the table.

"Why don't we try something different?" he said. "I'm gonna have you lay on your stomach, and I'm gonna have you do hamstring curls. You want to play ball again, right?"

It's almost like he was egging me on.

I lay down on my back and slowly rolled over on my stomach, being very careful of my leg. I saw him reach for one tube sock and then another and another and another and another, five of them that weighed five pounds each and another two-and-a-half-pound weight, a total of twenty-seven-and-a-half pounds. Then he wrapped them all on the back of my ankle with an ACE bandage. When he put the last one on, I looked back over my shoulder. It looked like I had a huge tumor on the lower part of my calf. I already knew I couldn't lift fifteen pounds, so how was I supposed to lift this?

"Do you want to play baseball again?" he asked me again.

"Yes, sir. It's my dream. It's my passion. I absolutely want to play again."

"Well, you got to work hard." Then he slapped me on the butt and left the room, leaving me alone to do the hamstring curls.

By this time, of course, I was determined to show him just how hard I could work. I grabbed the edge of the table with my hands for some leverage and tried to raise my foot and ankle from the table.

It didn't even move. I thought to myself, *"How can I possibly do this?"*

I remember taking a deep breath, then trying again, REALLY TRYING, and my foot started up from the table. It took all I had. I was grunting and sweating and I'm sure my face was beet red, but I somehow managed to lift my leg vertically from the table with those twenty-seven-and-a-half pounds of weights strapped to them.

Then I felt my leg starting to tremble. It just wasn't strong enough. The weight shifted violently. Instead of going back down to the table, my leg bent sideways out from the knee, off the table, as the rest of my body stayed pressed flat. My foot slammed against the floor and I heard my knee explode, the ligaments snapping, breaking loose like a leg from a roast chicken. The pain was unbelievable. Time seemed to stop. I screamed like an animal, as loud as I could.

A nurse and an aide rushed in. They saw my leg folded out in a direction no leg should ever be in and carefully lifted it back onto the table. I was sweating bullets and felt like throwing up, at first from the sound and now from the pain. One woman raced out to get ice while the other woman started to unwrap the Ace bandages. I was scared to death and began to realize that, not only should I not have been left alone, but I never should have had so much weight on my leg.

A minute or two later, the physical therapist comes in and tries to take over. He was completely cold. He didn't ask what was wrong and he didn't apologize. I was angry and scared and in pain. I felt like screaming at him, cussing him out, even though that wasn't allowed in our house. I kept on thinking, *"How could this guy be the head of physical therapy and still do this?"* I had trusted him. He showed no compassion whatsoever. My leg was already swelling and becoming discolored. I probably should have used a wheelchair, or even gone to the emergency room, but I just wanted to get out of there and away from him as fast as I could, tell my mom, see a doctor, and find out what the hell happened. The last thing I wanted to do was talk to this guy, because I was furious. The two women helped me off the table and onto my crutches.

Without enough muscle to support the weight, my lower leg had completely rotated as it fell. The noise I heard was the twisting and ripping of the ligaments and tissue that stabilized the knee. As I hobbled out on crutches, it didn't even feel like my lower leg was connected to my body anymore. As I lurched forward on the crutches, it swung back and forth like a dead weight. I couldn't even touch my toe to the ground to keep my balance. The car accident at McDonald's had been bad enough, but this felt worse—physically, emotionally, and—as I would soon learn, psychologically.

I stormed out with tears streaming down my face, some from the pain, some from fear, and some from shame and embarrassment—I was so fragile that I was actually worried almost as much about someone seeing me crying as I was about my leg. And it would not be long before nightmares about physical therapy would begin. My initial trauma from being struck by the car at McDonald's was at least doubled.

That's important to understand about PTSD. It can be caused by different events and manifest itself in different ways. Most people think PTSD occurs due to a single event—a roadside bomb going off or a car accident or an assault—and sometimes that is true. But PTSD can also result from multiple traumas—several accidents, like I had experienced—or even due to repeated, chronic traumas, such as what can take place during sexual abuse. And people who experience PTSD from one event can have that made worse by another traumatic event.

The initial reaction is always shock, the same reaction we all have to any terrible experience. In most people, that response fades away on its own, the event ends, and you calm down and find comfort from friends and family. PTSD comes about when that initial reaction doesn't shut off, as if the "flight or fright" response gets stuck, overriding your conscious control. It's a protection mechanism, the way your brain and body react to a terrible experience, by constantly reminding you how terrible it was so you don't put yourself in that position again. When I smelled McDonald's fries and had a flashback, it was my brain and body telling me, "Hey, something bad happened when you smelled this before," so I could avoid it. Of course, the fries had nothing to do with the accident. Still, the warning system never shuts off. Every time I smelled McDonald's fries, my body thought I was going to be struck by a car again.

That's what happened in physical therapy. The pain was traumatic and, due to my early accident, I was already isolating myself emotionally from other people and didn't seek out the comfort I should have. I was already hyper alert from the car accident and, as a result, my symptoms only got worse—more nightmares, more flashbacks, more things to worry about, more reactions to suppress.

I somehow made it to the car and very slowly and carefully managed to drive home. Every bump I hit made my leg hurt more and, when I made a turn, I had no control over my lower leg, it flopped around uncontrollably and caused still more pain. I made it in the house, called my mother at the church and told her what happened. She raced home and knew right away it was bad. She was distraught and kept saying, "I'm so sorry," over and over. Then she called the doctor and drove me right over.

I laid on his exam table and he started moving my leg. It moved way more than I had ever seen it move in my two other exams. He said I had "global instability," that it appeared that when my leg rotated and fell—basically, nearly everything that held my knee together had either torn loose or was severely damaged. He wouldn't know the full extent of my injuries until surgery. Once again, however, I had to wait for the swelling to subside before the surgery could be scheduled. I could barely move. We still had a hospital bed in the house from my first accident and I just lay in it for days, numbing myself with daytime television. The nightmares continued. But now, they weren't always of the car accident. Oh, I still had those too, only now I also sometimes woke up screaming as I felt my leg bounce off the floor. I would reach out for it to see if it was still there.

When I awoke in the recovery room after surgery, once again, I could feel the warm plaster cast on my leg. But I was also in excruciating pain, far worse than from my other surgeries. I thought, *"Holy crap, what did he do to me?"* I could see the IVs in my arm and knew I was on pain medication. The nurses came and injected something into the IV several times and, each time, said it would make me feel better, but it didn't.

A short time later, the surgeon came in. I asked "What did you do to fix me up, Doc? It really hurts."

The surgeon looked at me. He was calm and nice, but frank. He said the surgery took longer and was more involved than he had anticipated. He had expected to find serious damage, but nothing as severe as what he saw in there. The medial collateral ligament on the inside side of my knee, which had been damaged in the car accident and at school, had detached. The outside lateral collateral ligament on the outside of my knee, the ligament that connects the shin bone to the thigh bone, was no longer attached either. It was shredded, useless. There was also damage to the meniscus, the cartilage that cushions the knee, so the bones don't bang together. Fortunately, my anterior cruciate ligament, the ACL, was not completely torn, although it was damaged. Basically, all that was holding the bones of my lower leg to my upper leg was the ACL and soft tissue, my skin. Everything else had been torn up.

This made repairing my knee much more difficult and involved. He ended up basically doing "Tommy John" surgery on my leg, crafting new ligaments. In Tommy John surgery, which is done on the elbow and named after the first pitcher to successfully come back from the surgery, a new ligament is taken from a cadaver and put in the elbow. In my case, instead of using a ligament, he spliced both sides of my hamstring tendons, which usually run behind the knee, and stretched them to the side to stabilize the knee. The reason I was in so much pain was because he had to drill holes in my shin bone, pull those tendons through, tie them in a knot, and then pound half-inch staples into my bone to hold them in place. Essentially, he used the hamstring tendons to create a new ligament on each side of my knee to keep it stable and in place.

The hamstring, of course, isn't meant to do this and was stretched as far as it could be stretched. He said that, too, caused pain. He added that it would take incredible dedication and work for me to stretch out my hamstrings enough, so my knee would bend correctly. The more he talked, the more my mind raced with a hundred questions, including the biggest one. I remember wishing that my mother was with me so she could ask for me, but she wasn't yet allowed in the recovery room.

"Doc?" I said. "How soon before I can play baseball again? How soon 'til I can pitch?"

"You won't pitch again," he said. "You'll be lucky if you can walk normal." He raised his hands and wiggled two fingers on each, like he was making quotation marks in the air.

Chapter 4

*W*hen I heard that I couldn't pitch again, I just opened up. I couldn't stop the tears running down my face. I was so shocked and scared I didn't hear the rest of what he said.

Not being able to play baseball was devastating enough. Over the past six months, part of me had started to realize that was a possibility. I never considered that I might not be "normal" again, that I might never be able to walk and get around like everyone else. Until that point, I had looked at my injuries as something to get over—get through physical therapy and rehab and get back to normal. Now I was being told that I might have to live with a new normal, one that might include a limp or cane or wheelchair, a life without running or any of the things I'd dreamed of. My world suddenly got a lot more uncertain and a lot smaller.

I had never felt so alone. It was as if time had stopped. I was eighteen and it felt like my life was over. *If I couldn't walk normally, would I ever have a normal life? Would I have a girlfriend? What would I do for a living?* All these thoughts raced through my head, made worse by the fact that I was still woozy from the surgery. Yet, as I lay there, stunned and shocked, I also began, ever so slowly, to look ahead. After all, he had said I would be "lucky" to walk normally again. That didn't mean it was impossible. I was competitive enough that part of me heard those words and saw a challenge. Determined to prove him wrong, I set a goal. Maybe I couldn't play baseball, but I was going to do whatever it took to walk "normally" again. I'd show him. I wasn't going to allow that physical therapist to ruin my life.

What I faced now was my biggest challenge yet, not just physically, but emotionally. Setting a goal was one thing. Doing what was necessary to achieve that goal was something else entirely. I would have to go through the same routine I had already gone through twice before, a lengthy recovery with my leg in a full cast, followed by an even lengthier period of physical rehabilitation. Even though I was determined to prove the surgeon wrong, I couldn't do anything about that while bedridden.

I went through many lonely nights in the hospital, unable to sleep because of the pain. When I did nod off, I'd wake in a panic to the memory of a nightmare, my leg slamming onto the floor, the sound of my ligaments shredding, or a car racing toward me and running me over. I felt like the head therapist had stolen my dreams even more than the lady in the car; that had been an accident, whereas I felt the incident in PT was due more to neglect. When I returned home, my nightmares became even worse, and I would sleep with the TV on as loud as it could be without disturbing my mother.

I never mentioned the nightmares to anyone. I had no idea that they were common after traumatic accidents. There were times my mother heard me call out and came into my room at night, but it wasn't something we ever discussed. I must have put on a pretty good front. I think she knew I didn't want to talk about it and she probably didn't understand what was happening either. Day by day, I became more frightened and embarrassed by my symptoms.

I assumed that I was just weak and wondered why it was that I couldn't handle everything and move on.

Even baseball didn't provide any relief. For one thing, it was winter and there weren't any games to watch or listen to, and the strike during the 1981 season had disrupted everything. My Red Sox, after battling for the divisional title almost every season in the 1970s, slipped back and hadn't made the playoff for several years. Now, for the first time in my life, baseball didn't provide any comfort. All it did was remind me of what I could not do. My personal field of dreams had, literally, been taken over by a nightmare. I didn't want to deal with baseball. I didn't want to talk to anyone or do anything that would make me think of what my buddies were doing while away at school. I didn't feel sorry for myself as much as I just felt angry at the world. I would lie in bed and wonder, *"Why is this happening to me? I should be playing baseball."* I could have understood if I had had the opportunity and hadn't been good enough, but to have it taken away from me the way it was meant that I would never know. That tore me up.

Even though I had been through the recovery process before, this time, it was much more difficult. The physical pain was intense. Getting in and out of bed was even more challenging, And I was angry all the time. Each day, I became more isolated.

That's common for victims of PTSD. Although I didn't realize it then, one of the reasons I withdrew was to keep myself from experiencing anything that would trigger a flashback or risk another injury or force me to reveal my inner feelings. That's why so many PTSD victims pull away from people and isolate themselves, or self-medicate with drugs, alcohol, or other risky behaviors. It's to keep from confronting their own emotions. Isolation is the last thing in the world a victim of PTSD should do to themselves, but that's a symptom of the disorder. You stop trusting other people, you start thinking that they have no idea what you are experiencing and then, because you push everyone away when they do reach out, you mistrust them. You think they only reach out because of pity. You don't trust others or believe that they are sincere, so you withdraw even more. I reacted by staying home, nearly cutting off all contact with other people.

I had one good buddy at the time, but he had a serious girlfriend and spent most of his time with her. Many of my other friends were at school. Even when invited to do stuff on the weekends, I'd just say no. I was embarrassed to still be in a cast, worried I might fall and hurt my knee, and figured they were just being polite, that they really didn't want me around anyway.

Besides, they were busy, going forward in their lives, and I wasn't. I didn't have stories about school to share. The way I pushed everyone away made it easy for me to be left behind. Sometimes I would get a letter or a phone call, and that meant the world to me, but I didn't often reach back. I couldn't drive with the cast and was dependent on my mom or people from the church to go anywhere. I just wasn't social or very nice and I didn't want to talk to anyone. I was helpless and, at the same time, mad at the world. I trusted no one. That trust had been broken the moment my foot struck the floor. I didn't even trust the doctors anymore, not to mention physical therapists. I felt betrayed. From that time onward, anytime I met someone, they had to earn my trust.

This was the incident that changed my life. The other two had been bad enough, but at the time, I thought I would recover, at least physically. When my life got back to normal I thought I would get back to normal too. This felt permanent. I felt as if I had absolutely failed as a person, because now I had no chance of making the major leagues. For most of my life, I had dreamed of seeing my picture on a baseball card, of taking the mound at Fenway Park, of staring down a hitter, of being carried off the field after leading the Red Sox to a championship, just like Jim Lonborg had been carried off after the Sox clinched the pennant in 1967. Now all that was a fantasy. It would never happen.

My brothers and mom stayed upbeat and tried to keep my spirits up. My brothers called and visited often. They tried to tell me that, although I couldn't play baseball, there were other things I could do, that I had an opportunity now to discover another passion, and to make that my career. They would say, "Count your blessings. You're really fortunate right now, you have time to think about what you want to do and use your time wisely. Think about what you really have a passion for, find a career you love to do, reach for your dreams and never give up. Because so many people hate their jobs and can't wait to get home from work." By this time, Chip was working as an attorney in Colorado and Terry was a banker in Milwaukee. I knew they were right but, at the time, a lot of it went in one ear and out the other. I didn't think anyone understood what I was going through.

I had no idea what I wanted to do. There had been the vague notion of a business degree but no Plan B. I thought about trying to become a coach but knew that almost every coach or manager in the big leagues had played professionally and that every ex-minor leaguer, let alone every ex-major leaguer, already had their foot in the door at a higher level than I did. What was the chance of a Legion player ever making it to the majors as a coach? I didn't think that was possible. Other than a stubborn determination to walk normally again, I had no ambition.

I was in a cast ten or twelve weeks, a long time that felt even longer the third time around. It was good to finally get it off, but I was still on crutches. Every morning, I would do some stretches just to get around, and I still had to complete an extensive physical therapy program. Although I was determined to walk, after my last experience, I wasn't thrilled to get started, but I knew that I had to.

Needless to say, I didn't return to the same PT department as before. Still, when I went in the first time, I was mad at the world. I had to attend three or four times a week and it was seventy miles round-trip. My mother usually worked, so some volunteers from the church would take me. I thought of them as "sweet church Ladies," always nice and eager to talk. I was not. I dreaded being in the car all that time with a stranger. I should be riding around with a girl, going to the movies, not retirees going to PT.

I'm embarrassed to say that the first few times I attended PT I don't think I said hello or was even civil to the physical therapist who was trying to help me. I wasn't trying to be rude. I was just so withdrawn and felt so isolated, I wasn't nice at all. It was hard to be there and not think about the earlier incident and get angry.

This time around, I knew going in that my recovery period was going to be a lot longer than it would have been before. The first time, PT was mostly about building strength in my muscles that had atrophied from being in a cast and increasing the range of motion in my knee. Now, in addition to that, I had to really work hard to stretch out my hamstrings, so my leg would work normally. A lot of it involved stretches, like a hurdler's stretch, on the table. At first, I couldn't even go on the floor and do it. I had to overcome the fear that, as I stretched, the surgery would come undone and everything would pop loose and retract like a rubber band. Even though there was little chance of that happening in the kind of controlled treatment I was now undergoing, I was petrified. The entire process was slow and laborious. In addition to stretches and strength exercises—this time with very light weights and much more care—the therapists used massage to break down tissue and stretch out my muscles, alternating massage and heat to increase blood flow to the knee and promote healing.

Essentially, I had to learn to walk again. I had spent the better part of a year in bed, in a cast or a brace, and on crutches. I hadn't walked with my right leg in forever, and it's funny, but I had forgotten how. When I was strong enough to work on walking, a normal stride, walking so my foot landed heel to toe no longer felt right. My right leg wanted to go the opposite way, toe to heel. I remember walking in front of a mirror, and it just didn't make sense. It was tedious and took weeks. I made progress, but it was so slow and frustrating. It didn't help that I was the youngest person, by far, undergoing therapy. My appointments were always in the late morning and there were no other high school or college-aged patients I could hang out and talk with. Nearly all the patients were elderly, rehabbing from hip and joint replacements. I didn't think anyone there could relate to what was going on with me, or that I shared anything with them.

Still, I tried to adapt. I really wanted to walk. I guess it came from being athletic but, in my mind, I tried to turn everything into a game. I challenged myself to do more each time than I had before, to find something positive to hang onto, no matter how trivial, whether it was one more rep of an exercise or another degree of movement in the bend of my knee. They would measure that with a gauge and I always tried to keep track. It was a big deal to gain even a single degree in my range of motion.

Back home, I was timid and withdrawn. Although it was easier to get around without the cast, I was increasingly isolated. All I could do was dwell on what I didn't have or what I had lost.

One day at therapy, I was with all these older people, looking around and feeling sorry for myself, thinking, "These people can't possibly understand what I'm going through. They've lived full lives, while I'm eighteen and have already had three knee surgeries in the past year." Then I noticed someone who I had never seen before. He was younger than the rest of the patients, but older than me. He had short, dark hair parted on the side and an athletic build that reminded me of a wrestler. I was in the front of the room and he was toward the back. Then I noticed something else: he did not have legs. Both had been amputated below the knee and you could tell it had happened recently. He was on a table, getting a massage.

That's not what made him stand out. What set him apart was his attitude. The whole time he's getting worked on, he's joking with the therapist, laughing, engaging the other older patients in conversation. He was so positive, so outgoing, he just lit up the room. I was all the way over on the other side and he was even making me feel better. When I overheard him say how *happy* he was, I couldn't believe it. How could this guy without legs, a bilateral amputee below the knees, have such a great attitude?

For the first time in a long time, I started to get some perspective. Now, suddenly, all the stuff my brothers and my mother had been telling me made sense. It really made me rethink my situation and how I was interacting with people. As I watched him, I realized that, as challenging as my situation was, many other people were in much worse shape. I had been feeling sorry for myself when, in reality, almost everyone at PT was having at least as hard a time as me, yet I was acting like I had it worse than anyone.

Holy crap, I thought. *I better start realizing how lucky I am*. Right in front of me was an example of everything my brothers and my mother had been telling me: it could always be worse. For months, they had been telling me to keep reaching for my dreams, not to give up, not to quit, to focus us on what I could do instead of what I couldn't, and to be happy with what I have.

I began thinking more about what I did have than what I did not. After all, I had my legs. I had my arms and hands. I had my whole life in front of me, yet I hadn't appreciated it. I decided to do all I could to move forward with my life, to overcome my fears of the future by taking charge of the present.

That is a moment I'll never forget, one that changed my life. It was a great learning opportunity. The man with no legs was a living, breathing example right in front of me of how to go forward, of how to approach the rest of my life. I remember thinking to myself, "I have nothing to complain about. I better suck it up, and I'm going to use this as a stepping stone." Self-confidence is a powerful force. He inspired me and, for the first time since my accident, I began to feel empowered.

I wish I would have spoken to him, but I never did and, in fact, I never saw him again. He must have normally been scheduled to come in at a different time and, for some reason, on this day, had to change the time of his appointment. I'm glad he did. My whole attitude toward physical therapy changed. For the first time, it seemed as if I noticed the other people around me. I started to look forward to seeing them, to say hello and joke around with them as well. I learned that positive energy was infectious and, ever so slowly, I started to climb out of the shell I had made for myself.

Still, I was battling the worst physical pain I had ever experienced, combined with increasingly debilitating flashbacks and night terrors. I wasn't sleeping well. One night, around 3:00 a.m., I was lying awake in pain, flipping channels to try to distract myself when I came across a TV evangelist. For some reason, I paused. Just a few seconds later, the minister said, "Let's all pray for David Mellor in Piqua, Ohio, who is facing a tough time in his life and needs our support." I thought I was hearing things. I called to my Mom and woke her up to see if she had any idea how that minister had heard of me. She came rushing in to see me, but she didn't know what I was talking about. I still do not know why I stopped on that station, but I feel it was a sign from God to hang in there.

As an assistant to the pastor, my Mom was very active in our church. When I was in high school, I was a Junior Trustee and, over the next few years, became a Trustee and a Deacon. I began to learn more about my faith and how to help people. My belief in a higher power helped me realize that, despite every setback, I would get better if I worked hard at it. I knew I wouldn't heal overnight but I put my trust in my faith and my philosophy to take "one base at a time," to use each triumph, no matter how small, to give me strength to take on the next challenge, providing me with yet another reason to keep the faith. I consider myself a spiritual person and believe that God has a bigger plan for me. Despite my physical and emotional issues, that gave me a reason to go on. I had important work to do.

My faith and change in attitude didn't have much of an impact on my emerging PTSD symptoms. On the outside, I tried to be happy-go-lucky, like I didn't have a care in the world, and be the funny guy at the party. Over time, I got better at it and, in many ways, learned to live a false life, to pretend that nothing was wrong, even though I was constantly worried about someone noticing that I was having a flashback and that I might not be able to control my emotions. I always tried to defuse it with something else. If I felt like something was happening, I'd try to excuse myself, change the subject, do something stupid, anything to distract people from recognizing that my heart was racing, and I was in a panic. I'm sure there were times people wondered what the hell was going on with me because I would do or say things that didn't make much sense.

At least, in terms of my physical challenges, I now had a way to cope and move forward. It made a huge difference. Had I not learned how to do that and build a new life, at least on the outside, I don't know what would have happened. Although I still had invisible scars on the inside, I now had a strategy to deal with the visible scars on my knee. This period of rehabilitation lasted all spring and into the summer. Instead of dreading those sessions, I looked forward to seeing my physical therapist and the other outpatients, to focus on each new task and goal. Once I regained my strength and range of motion, I began to learn to walk and put weight on my leg, wearing a series of braces similar to those once worn by quarterback Joe Namath, and designed at the same hospital, because the anatomy of my knee had changed and required extra support. Some of the braces required Velcro straps. They made a great deal of noise every time I had to adjust them, and that made me self-conscious. I would undo the straps as slowly and quietly as possible. I slowly transitioned to a cane and in May of 1982—I stopped using crutches for what I hoped was the last time.

I could walk around my house without my cane—slowly, and still with a big limp. But, because I still felt nervous around people and worried that someone might bump into me and knock me over, I was uncomfortable in crowds. I used the cane whenever I went out for protection and avoided places where there were a lot of people. Yet, with increased mobility, I started interacting more with old friends, sometimes even going out on my own.

Sometimes I'd be out in a crowd and a stranger would refer to me as "Festus," the physically challenged character in the TV western *Gunsmoke*, or "Hopalong." I'd try very hard not to limp, and I'd laugh, but inside I was sensitive and, at times, felt bullied. Sometimes I'd be walking with a group and someone would say something about how I was slowing them down, which made me ashamed and even more self-conscious.

When the weather was warm, I often wore shorts. My scars were nearly a foot long, red and purplish, sunken in, and very visible.

People sometimes stared or made smart remarks. As hard as I was trying to come out of my shell, such comments pushed me back in. So, in addition to worrying about flashbacks, I now I worried about how others viewed me. I was still unable to work or go to school, so I already felt different.

I was proud of what I'd accomplished but realized I wasn't walking like everybody else, like normal, and some people thought it was their business to make sure I knew that. Now I look at my scars as something I've earned, that I'm proud of. But it has taken me many years to feel that way. If anyone asks about my scars today or I see them looking, I'll tell the story, but, back then, I'd either pretend it didn't happen, crack a joke, or make up some outlandish story and act like it didn't bother me. I did that for thirty years until I went through therapy for my PTSD.

My experiences in physical therapy gave me a good understanding of what physical therapy could accomplish when it was done the right way and the consequences when it was not. As I watched therapists help people recover from injuries and return to living full lives, I also learned the difference between a caring professional and one who was not so concerned with their patients. Effective physical therapy wasn't just a series of exercises but required a knowledgeable and caring provider a patient could trust. As a result, I began to develop an interest in the field. With the advice from my family to find a passion echoing in my head, the notion of helping people resume an active life was appealing. I knew teams employed trainers and phys-ical therapists and specialists, and I thought that, if I studied sports medicine, I might, one day, be able to get a job with the training staff of a major league ballclub. That fall, I was finally healthy enough to enroll in a few classes at the local community college, studying anatomy and physiology to learn more about the human body. Ever so slowly, my dream about making it to the majors was changing.

I knew I wouldn't do so as a player, but I now realized there were other paths to Fenway Park. As soon as I was healthy, I was determined to take some big steps in that direction.

Chip was working in Denver as an attorney with a law foundation. A young man clerking in his office had grown up on the family cattle ranch, then the largest in the country, the Spann Ranch, in Gunnison, Colorado. They also operated two "satellite" ranches in Crested Butte and the family had been in the ranching business for over a hundred years. They kept thousands of head of cattle, herding them from pasture to pasture from the spring to the fall, and then rounding them up every winter, caring for the calves, doing everything you imagine cowboys and ranch hands do on a ranch.

My brother must have told him about my accidents and about how hard I'd been working to regain my strength and confidence. The clerk told Chip that, if my leg was strong enough, he could set it up, so I could come up there and work on the ranch later that summer. He must have sensed that it would provide me with a goal to work toward during PT, and that working on the ranch would build my self-confidence. When Chip told me, I was thrilled. I felt like I had been cooped up at home just doing PT forever. And, although I had been working hard, having a tangible goal made it so much easier to push myself at PT. I felt like I was getting ready for a big game or something.

I'd never really done any kind of hard physical labor and the idea of working on the ranch was thrilling. By mid-summer, I was off crutches and only used my cane once in a while. Although I still wore a heavy brace for extra support and wasn't quite "normal," I had progressed to the point where I could begin to live a much more normal life. My doctor was completely on board. He monitored me closely and thought I had gained enough strength to go out there and work, although he cautioned me to be careful, to take my cane, and to back off if my knee started to bother me. But the fact that he thought I could do it gave me confidence. That was something I really needed. After a year of inactivity, my confidence needed all the help it could get.

I could not have been more excited and drove myself halfway across the country to get there. The trip took two days and the miles on the road just flew by. I stopped by to see Chip before going to the ranch. My destination was Crested Butte. When I arrived, I could not believe how beautiful it was, ranches tucked into valleys surrounded by the Rocky Mountains. It looked like something from television or a movie. I moved in with the owner's son on a satellite ranch.

From the first morning, it was an incredible, once-in-a-lifetime experience. I was just a small-town kid and, apart from cutting grass, I really didn't have any mechanical ability or experience doing physical labor. Yet I was treated like I was just another ranch hand right from the start. All the guys treated me like I was one of them, which meant I was the butt of every joke and insult they could throw my way. But it was all good-natured, to see if I could take it, a way to let me know I belonged.

Every day started at sunrise. We'd work until the early afternoon, take a break for an enormous steak lunch, then work until sunset. I remember, that first day, we were bailing hay. I don't think I had ever worked so hard in my life. I started out wearing a T-shirt and jeans and, in the thin mountain air, the temperature must have got up to about 85 degrees. I was drenched with sweat. But, later that afternoon, as the sun dropped behind the mountains, it got cold—and quick. I didn't know it yet, but Crested Butte often had the widest daily temperature range in the entire country. It could be searing hot all day and then drop to almost freezing at night. All of a sudden, I would be shivering and see everyone else pulling on sweatshirts and putting on down vests. Of course, no one had told me to bring warmer clothes; they had set me up and I froze the rest of the day. I realized it was going to be a fun time, but I had to keep on my toes. The next morning, I was helping work on an engine and they sent me under it to undo a drain plug. I didn't know it was full of oil and, as soon as I loosened the plug, oil came pouring out all over me. Even though I was from a small town, they thought I was this young city slicker and the cowboys and ranch hands had some fun with that. Yet, at the same time, I could tell that they liked me. Although I couldn't ride a horse because of my knee, each day, I became more comfortable—and learned more and became better at helping out. It was almost like being on a team again, the same kind of close camaraderie. I was working hard and proud that, despite my knee, I was able to keep up and do my share.

I was working harder than I had ever worked in my entire life, before or since, and I loved every minute of it. Hard work, but with a lot of joking and laughing too. One of the guys that worked on the ranch was the nephew of Ted Kluszewski, the star first baseman of the Cincinnati Reds in the 1950s and early '60s. He was a big baseball fan and we would talk often. It was a wonderful environment for me. I was starting to trust people again, and was working so hard and getting so physically tired each day that I didn't stay so focused on avoiding flashbacks, and, although I still had nightmares, I fell asleep more easily. Knowing that I could keep up with these hardened ranch hands made me feel like I was a man. At least I was getting a chance to grow up and be independent, like my friends.

Every day delivered another incredible experience. After a week or so, I took part in a cattle drive, herding hundreds of head of cattle from the main ranch to Crested Butte. The cowboys would ride the fence line up in the mountains and herd the cattle down into the valley. We were allowed to drive the cattle right down the highway, State Route 50. It was only a two-lane road but, during a cattle drive, the cattle have the right of way. If a car hit a cow or a bull, they had to buy it and compensate the ranch but, if a bull scratched or dented a car, it wasn't considered the ranchers' fault. This was the west. The cattle ruled.

I rode in a truck following along behind and it was incredible to see all these cattle taking over the road while funneling down into the valley. My confidence soared. I had adapted to wearing the brace and there were times I almost forgot that I still had to wear it. That didn't mean I could run or jump, but it meant the world to me knowing I could hold my own with these tough cowhands. My self-esteem started to skyrocket. After all, I was doing something many "normal" people couldn't. I felt that, if I could work as a ranch hand, I could do just about anything.

Maybe I should have been more cautious. One day on a cattle drive, one of the hands noticed an old bull was going blind. They separated it from the herd and put it in a corral on the ranch. The next day, they decided to take it away and backed a truck to the end of a chute in the corral. The cowboys tried to herd the bull into the back of the truck, but he was stubborn, and dug his hooves in just short of the truck. I was watching all these cowboys behind the bull pushing and shoving, and then, all of a sudden, one called out, "Hey, Dave! Hop in there and grab that bull by the horns and pull him into the truck while we push!"

I thought they were joking, that this was another setup, and I was starting to get wise to that. "No way," I said, "there's no way I'm getting in there with this big bull. I'm not stupid. You guys are setting me up again." No one laughed. They were serious. I was one of the guys now and they needed my help.

"Get the hell in there, Dave!" someone yelled. So I climbed in, grabbed the bull by the horns, and started to pull as they all pushed. Before I knew it, that old bull gave a big grunt, lowered his head, bellowed again, blew snot out of his nose, then raised his head up fast, like a bull in the rodeo. His head caught me square in the chest and sent me flying. As soon as I hit the ground, I felt what was now a too-familiar sensation in my knee. Despite the brace, I had blown it out again. No one knew that, though, and everyone was laughing. I was so embarrassed. I scrambled to get up, hoping no one noticed I was hurt and praying that, somehow, I'd be able to continue but, as soon as I tried to put weight on my knee, I knew it was bad. "Oh, no," I thought, "my leg's hurt. It's not just sore. Something's not right here."

I tried to tough it out the rest of the day, but it was pretty clear that I was hurting, and the guys soon took me back to the ranch. The son of the owner could not have been nicer. We put ice on my knee to see if that would help. They knew the owners of a nearby resort and, over the next few days, I was allowed to use the Jacuzzi there, but it soon became obvious that something was seriously wrong. When I contacted Chip in Denver, he asked if I wanted to see a surgeon there or go on back home. I decided to go back to Ohio.

The one-legged drive back across the country was as tedious now as it had been exciting just a few weeks before. I struggled with a wide range of emotions as the middle part of the country flew past. In the end, although I was extremely disappointed, I knew I just had to continue forward. I would have to get this fixed and then regain my strength and mobility. I'd done it before and could do it again. My faith would give me the strength to continue. What choice did I have?

My doctor determined that some of the tendon transfer had broken loose, and I soon had more surgery to reconnect it. It wasn't quite as involved as my earlier surgeries, but it still required a long rehabilitation. Fortunately, it didn't cause new nightmares or flashbacks. That's the interesting thing about PTSD—it's not like, once you have PTSD, every bad experience is going to make it worse or cause a new episode. The accidents at McDonald's and at PT were out of my control, caused by other people and, in each case, the accident stretched out over time—it wasn't just the accident that was traumatic; it the immediate aftermath as well. In each case, I'd been left alone and was powerless. At McDonald's, I had been pinned against the building for several minutes and, in PT, it had taken some time before the aids heard my screams and came in to help me.

That's part of the reason those incidents resulted in PTSD. In each case, I didn't know what would happen next and felt powerless. However, when I slipped in the dorm room and was struck by the bull, those were genuine accidents I couldn't blame on anyone. Each of those incidents happened quickly and I received immediate support from those around me. They were tough experiences— and painful—but they didn't make me feel hopeless. As such, they weren't as traumatic as the others. After I slipped in the dorm room and was hit by the bull, I already knew what the recovery process was like. Although they certainly didn't help my PTSD symptoms, they didn't cause new nightmares or trigger new kinds of flashbacks. When I saw cattle afterwards, I just saw an animal, I didn't relive the experience of being hit by the bull.

After the surgery, I felt as if I was running in place, except I couldn't run, and I wasn't going forward much. Unfortunately, this was becoming "normal" to me.

Chapter 5

I was bound and determined to feel better again. I stuck with my "one-base-at-a-time" philosophy. You know, you can't hit a five-run homer, you just have to keep moving around the bases. I turned the smallest challenge, from getting up and walking to the bathroom to doing one more set in physical therapy, into a game I was determined to win.

I became so focused on PT and was so afraid of blowing my knee out again that, once again, I began to withdraw from all my friends and became hypervigilant. When my buddies would call and ask if I wanted to go out or hang out at somebody's house, I was almost paranoid that somebody'd bump into my leg. I usually came up with some excuse to stay home.

My friend, Jim, had a very serious girlfriend at the time, Joanie, who later became his wife. In October, he called me and said, "You need to go out and have some fun. All you do is go to physical therapy and go to school, and then you go home." I told him that I was fine, that I didn't need to go out, but Jim and Joanie were persistent. She worked at a flower shop with another young woman and wanted the four of us to go out on a double date. Now, this was really frightening. I could face physical therapy, but the idea of a blind double date scared me to death.

I told them, "I'm not going to go out on any kind of double date. I don't even know who this person is. Thanks for thinking of me, but I'm fine."

Of course, I wasn't. I was shy anyway, but the accident had made me even more so. I hadn't had a date since my first accident, and I didn't want to be the fourth wheel—a broken wheel at that, limping around with a cane. What girl my age wanted to date a guy like that? What kind of first impression would that make?

Jim and Joanie just wouldn't let up and, over the next few days, they wore me down. I think I finally agreed just to get them off my back. Jim even told me that, if we went out and I wasn't having a good time, "All you got to do is say your knee hurts and I promise we'll stop." So I agreed.

A few days later, we all met at Joanie's house. I remember being in the kitchen with Jim and Joanie's father when Joanie and her friend, Denise, walked in. I was awestruck. Denise was so pretty. We all started talking and she was so nice and kind and non-judgmental. I was so sensitive that I thought everyone saw my challenges first, but here was this girl, a very pretty girl, smiling at me and chatting. She didn't seem to see my brace or my cane, she just saw me. All I saw was her. It must have been all over my face. Joanie's father noticed and, after a moment, he kind of smirked and said, "Well, Dave, does your leg still hurt?" Everyone laughed. I was embarrassed, but he was right. For the first time in a long time, I wasn't thinking about my leg.

The four of us went out to eat and I was so taken I can't even remember the name of the restaurant. All I know was that it was

Mexican. Denise was easy to talk to and I couldn't take my eyes off of her. Then we decided to go to a club that had a band. I wasn't comfortable at all being in public with my brace and my cane, much less in a crowded club, where people are dancing, drinking, milling around, and jostling back and forth. Yet here I was, in public, in a room teeming with people. I was having so much fun being with Denise, I just about forgot everything else.

Then Denise asked me to dance. How could I say no? At that point, I would have done just about anything she asked. So I got out on the dance floor, in the middle of the crowd, with my cane and my leg brace, and I danced. Not very well, I'm sure, but I figured if I was with Denise, no one would be looking at me anyway.

I was completely smitten. We started dating right away and, for the first time since my accident, I almost felt normal. My life still wasn't perfect, and neither was my knee but, after meeting Denise, I at least felt as if I was moving forward and looking ahead. For the rest of that fall and winter and into the spring and summer, I continued going to rehab, stretching out my hamstring and building strength. I was doing it for myself but, at a certain point, I also realized I was doing it for something more. I was doing it for Denise, so we might have a future together, and for my family, to make them proud. As soon as my knee allowed it, I wanted to go to college full time and study physical therapy.

Baseball was never far from my mind and, by the spring, I was getting around well enough that I helped coach the local American Legion team. I had to be careful—I still wore a big metal and Velcro brace on my knee, but I was able to move around and help out with drills and things like that. It was nice to be on a ballfield again, but it was also hard. It wasn't like playing, and I'd be lying if I said there were not times at practice or during games when I almost forgot I was coaching and would imagine I was on the mound again, pitching. Despite my improved attitude and determination, I still dreaded trying to go to sleep. The nightmares were just as bad as ever and I remained hypervigilant about flashbacks, but now that I was out of my shell, I guess I was getting better at hiding my symptoms too. It made it easier to get through each day, but it wasn't like I was fixing the problem. I still didn't even know I had a problem, really, at least the kind that could be fixed. I still just thought I was messed up inside, something I wanted to keep hidden from Denise and everyone else.

I was still gaining strength that summer when I finally applied to re-enter college, this time at Ohio State. The university had a very advanced program in Athletic Training and Physical Therapy, and the field was starting to bridge the gap between sports and medicine. The head football trainer, Billy Hill, was heavily involved in the program and had a national reputation for mentoring team trainers. I thought it would be awesome to get a degree as a trainer and physical therapist and then go to work for a major league team. One way or another, I was going to make it to the major leagues. Unfortunately, I wasn't the only prospective student impressed with the program. Although I applied and was accepted to start school in the fall of 1984, the PT and athletic training program was already filled up. If that's what I wanted to study, I would be wait-listed until the following year.

I felt like the rug had been pulled out from under me. Life was passing me by and this was just one more sign that I was falling behind. My brothers and my mom had always told me to find something I was really going to love and be passionate about, and I had, but now I couldn't pursue it. I didn't want to wait another year to get started. I asked myself, "What do you really, really like to do.

What do you really love?" Maybe I could study something else. I started listing all the things I enjoyed. I loved being outside, I loved nature, and I didn't think I'd want to be stuck in an office all the time. Science was a subject I enjoyed in school and I still loved baseball. And I had always enjoyed mowing the grass and taking care of people's lawns.

Then I started to think: Hmm. Baseball fields are covered with grass—well, many of them were at the time—and those that did have grass fields were all outdoors. All of a sudden, I could see it, like a light bulb going off. Somebody has to take care of the field, right? I could be a groundskeeper! Yeah, that was it! I would become a groundskeeper. That's how I would make the major leagues. I might never be able to step on the field as a player, but I could be responsible for the upkeep of every inch of the field.

I looked into the programs at Ohio State and saw that they offered a Bachelor of Science degree in Agriculture specializing in Agronomy (the science of soil management and crop production) and Landscape Horticulture/Turf Grass Management. That's the background I would need if I wanted to enter the field. Although I felt like the world's oldest freshman, when I started at Ohio State that fall, I finally had a plan. At last, I had finally discovered another path that could lead me to the major leagues. Now all I had to do was the work!

I lived in a dorm room with two other students. They were both eighteen and I was twenty-one, yet when Denise and my Mom dropped me off that first day, I was filled with anxiety. Once again, I was afraid that they would find out about my nightmares or that someone would show up with a bag of French Fries from McDonald's and that would trigger a flashback or panic attack. As excited as I was about getting to school, I was just as concerned about how

I would be able to keep myself together. I still fell asleep to the television, I had a tiny portable I watched every night. Looking back, I think the only reason I was able to keep going was the fact that I was on a mission. I wanted to get done with school as quickly as I could, so that Denise and I could move on with our lives. I already knew I wanted to marry her, but I didn't want to get engaged until I was out of school.

Chip and Terry told me that, if I was serious about becoming a groundskeeper, I should reach out to some major league groundskeepers, tell them about my plans, ask for their advice, and see if they have any suggestions on how to get my foot in the door. That way, in a few years when I was looking for work, they might remember me and help me get a job. After all, there were only thirty teams in the major leagues, and thirty head groundskeepers, each with a staff of their own. There were more than seven hundred players in the major leagues. I didn't realize it at the time, but the odds of making it to the majors as a head groundskeeper were probably about the same as making it as a player—not very good!

I took their advice. I did some research and wrote every head groundskeeper in the major leagues, even those whose fields were artificial turf. The Expos groundskeeper wrote back and explained to me that they were required to give preference to Canadian workers, but I received more positive responses from Sam Newpher of the Braves, Roger Brossard of the White Sox, Joe Mooney of the Red Sox, and the Kansas City Royal's George Toma. I didn't realize it then but, eventually, all four would become dear friends. Newpher worked for the Braves for nearly two decades before moving on to take care of the grounds at the Daytona race track. I called there one day to compliment them on a mowing design, and Sam actually remembered my letter to him. He thanked me for calling and told me that the mowing pattern was one that Cacky had created for my book, *Picture Perfect*. He also knew that Cacky had come up with the design we used at Fenway. He recently retired, but not before hiring my dear friend and colleague at Fenway, Jason Griffeth.

Roger Brossard started working for the White Sox as a teenager, and both his father and grandfather had also been groundskeepers. He was so well-respected that, when Saudi Arabia wanted to build a natural grass soccer field in the middle of the desert, they hired him. In the business, he was known affectionately as "the Sodfather."

Joe Mooney was responsible for Fenway Park and was known as someone who watched over his field like a hawk, taking care of every detail. He got his start in the minor leagues in Scranton, Pennsylvania, and worked at RFK Stadium in Washington when both Ted Williams and Vince Lombardi were there. He joined the Red Sox in 1971, just as Fenway Park began to be recognized as a piece of living history. Although I would later learn that his bark was much louder than his bite, anyone who had ever spent any time at Fenway knew that Joe was exceptionally protective of the field.

George Toma also got his start as a groundkeeper in the minor leagues, in Wilkes Barre, Pennsylvania. He then served in the military in Korea before being hired in Kansas City. He was later hired to prepare the field for the first Super Bowl and performed that duty at every subsequent Super Bowl until he retired. He also served as head groundskeeper for several Olympic Games and the 1994 World Cup.

In my letters, I introduced myself to each man, briefly explained my situation and shared my plans to attend Ohio State to study landscape horticulture and agronomy. I told them my dream was to be a Head Groundskeeper in the major leagues and asked for their guidance, for the best way to reach my dream.

I hadn't expected to hear back from any of them. I figured they probably received dozens of letters like mine each year, and they would be way too busy to take the time to respond to some college kid in Ohio. I didn't realize it at the time, but I was entering the field at an exciting time. Most of the groundskeepers, like Newpher, Brossard, Mooney, and Toma, had learned their trade by trial and error, and by picking the brains of their peers. Brossard had studied agronomy in college, but all of them knew what they were doing and were successful, and as a result of their pioneering work, the field was now being regarded as a bona fide profession. This was no longer an area where you could just walk up with general landscaping experience. Prestigious golf clubs were requiring college degrees for employment and all sorts of other facilities were in need of professionals to take care of their grounds. Colleges were responding by creating course programs designed to fill that need. There was much more to being a groundskeeper than cutting grass. Different grasses and different soils all had different properties and you had to take into consideration the weather and field use along with a host of other factors. Golf courses and stadiums cost millions of dollars and professional athletes were earning millions as well. No one wanted an investment ruined by a poor field or have an athlete injured because the field wasn't cared for properly. As it turned out, I was entering the field at just the right time. Eventually, I became the first student at Ohio State to go into sports turf management.

A few weeks after sending the letters, I was surprised to hear back from all four men. All were supportive and encouraged me to study Agronomy and to try to gain practical experience through internships and work during the summer. George Toma's response was particularly impressive. Not only was his letter long—sixteen pages—but he had written it on Thanksgiving Day. I couldn't believe how generous that was, that a man like him would take the time on a holiday to write such a considerate letter to someone he'd never met. I have never forgotten their generosity. I did not realize at the time but being closed out from pursuing physical therapy school at school proved to be another blessing in disguise.

While I was motivated before, I was even more motivated after receiving those letters. I was studying hard, taking the basics, like chemistry, and eager to get going. My brother Terry was still working as a banker in Milwaukee and he told me that, if I could ever get a job with the Brewers, he would let me stay with him. Dreams like that made it easier for me to go on.

Of course, I was also a college student, and didn't study all the time. Although I wasn't a big partier, I liked to go out with my friends and have a good time, just like everyone else. Even though I still wore my brace, I tried to do all the things every other college kid did.

School was going well that fall. We were on the quarter system, and it had just gotten cold. I had a late afternoon class, and it was almost dusk when I started walking back to the dorm with some friends, going down a little side street that was on a bit of an incline. The light was bad and we couldn't see very well. What looked like a bit of wet pavement was actually black ice. We were yukking it up, joking around and not paying attention when the person to my right lost his footing. Then it was like something from the Three Stooges. He started slipping and sliding and fell, causing a chain reaction. Suddenly, we were all slipping, losing our balance and banging into one another. He knocked me down and I knocked down the person on the other side of me. Then there were three or four of us on the ground, legs in the air and schoolbooks scattered everywhere.

My right leg somehow ended up going behind me. I swear it felt like it ended up somewhere close to my head. It was just a freak thing, but the fall was so sudden and violent that the Velcro straps on my brace came undone. Right then, I knew my knee was screwed. Everybody was down in a heap laughing—it was kind of funny the way we all fell at once—and I tried to laugh it off as well because I was so embarrassed. But the pain and disappointment were so bad I could feel my eyes filling with tears. As my friends helped me back to my feet, they noticed. Even after I reattached the brace, I could barely put weight on it. I remember I had to hold onto a handrail along the sidewalk just to shuffle along.

I knew my knee wasn't right. The next day, I went back to see my doctor in Dayton and, sure enough, I had torn parts of the tendon transfer, just as I had done in Colorado, but in a slightly different spot—the scar tissue from the earlier injury had actually strengthened it in that spot, so it tore somewhere else. I had to have more surgery. I couldn't even finish the quarter.

Once again, I had to put my life on hold, withdraw from school, pack everything up, return home, have surgery and begin another laborious round of physical therapy. I ended up having two surgeries because, a short time later, one of the staples they had put in my shin to help hold the tendon in place started to come loose, so the surgeon had to go back in and fix that.

Somehow, I was even more focused than ever to recover and get back to Ohio State. I had physical therapy three times a week for months and, once again, I had to depend on friends of the family to drive me back and forth as I slowly recovered. When friends told me I was jinxed, I just told them this was another challenge and that I would become a stronger person because of it. I believed that. I had to believe that.

Throughout this entire time, Denise was amazing. She's been pretty amazing since I first met her. It would have been easy for her to have decided I was too much trouble, but she never did. She always seemed to know when and how to motivate me. She is a gift from God.

I finally made it back to Ohio State in the fall of 1985. But I was so far behind I was impatient and wanted to finish as quickly as possible. I met with the Assistant Dean of Students, Dr. Ray Miller, and told him I was dedicated to work hard and wanted to graduate as quickly as possible to make up for the three years of college I had lost to the injuries and surgeries. He told me that twelve to eighteen credit hours per quarter were considered a normal, full-time course load. I asked him, "What are the most credit hours I could take per quarter?" He said I could take up to twenty-seven credit hours per quarter, but only if I kept a B average.

That's what I decided to do. While most students were taking three or four classes at a time, I was taking five and six classes. In addition to that, to earn extra money and help pay for college, I got a part-time job on the greens crew at the Scioto Country Club in Upper Arlington, Ohio, just a short drive from campus. That's the course Jack Nicklaus grew up playing on and has hosted the US Open.

Many weekday mornings, I began work at 5:00 a.m., mowing greens and fairways for a couple hours before starting class at 8:00 a.m. And, sometimes, my last class didn't finish until 9:00 p.m. It was tough to juggle my classes, work, and study time, but I put myself on a strict schedule to make the most of my opportunities. On weekends, I sometimes put in more hours at the Country Club, and I was active in several university clubs as well. I was completely focused on getting my degree and getting to the majors.

It wasn't all positive. I realize now that I was also working hard to keep from confronting the symptoms of PTSD. If I worked all the time, that didn't leave me much time to worry about having flashbacks. And, if I was exhausted every evening, it made it easier to go to sleep, despite my fear of nightmares. And, if I worked all the time, I didn't have to discuss my feelings with Denise or anyone else. If I worked all the time—and was successful—it was easy to convince myself that I was okay, that I wasn't messed up. By working hard, I was trying to prove to myself that I was fine.

I know now that many PTSD victims react in a similar way. Although PTSD can lead some people to withdraw completely, it can cause others to become workaholics, to hide in their work. It's not uncommon for some PTSD victims to become high achievers and work every waking hour. Between work and school, I sometimes worked more than a hundred hours a week, sixteen, eighteen hours a day, literally doing nothing more than working, studying, and sleeping, all in an attempt to keep my mind off my problems. The last thing I wanted was to be alone with my own thoughts. In the short term, it helped me reach my dream, but it also became a habit that would eventually put distance between me and my family. While there is nothing wrong with having a strong work ethic, learning not to work all the time has been a part of my recovery.

After Terry told me I could stay with him if I could get an internship with the Milwaukee Brewers, I focused on that like a laser. He helped me put together a resume and worked on a cover letter to send to the Brewers, and I peppered them with applications and phone calls. I think they finally just got tired of hearing from me. Late in the spring, they called and said they would like to hire me, but the only open position was part-time, a day-of-game position. I eagerly accepted and called Terry to tell him I was coming to Milwaukee. I was going to the big leagues.

Milwaukee's County Stadium was an older, utilitarian stadium then used by both the Brewers and the Green Bay Packers. I couldn't believe I would have the opportunity to work on the same field where Hank Aaron and Eddie Mathews once played ball or where Bart Starr and Ray Nitschke starred for the Packers. County Stadium might not have been the most glamorous ballpark in the country, but it was the big leagues, and that was all that mattered to me.

On my first day, I could hardly believe I was finally working on an MLB field. The Brewers had been in the World Series a few years before and their lineup still featured stars like Paul Molitor and Robin Yount. It was thrilling to see big league players up close, but it was quickly explained to me that my job was to do as I was told and to allow the players to do their job. When you work for a major league team in any capacity, you quickly realize that the ballplayers are there to work, to do their job. It's unprofessional to bother them, particularly when you're a part-timer working his first game.

Before the game, I helped set up the field for BP, pulled the hose to water the field, moved equipment, and carried rakes and shovels, anything I was asked. Just before the game was scheduled to begin, and our pre-game duties were over, I asked my boss what he wanted me to do next. He told me to wait on the warning track by the camera pit in foul territory, and he would let me know. I stood there waiting, and soon noticed that everyone else on the grounds crew had left the field. In the outfield, a gate opened, and an elephant appeared, lumbering onto the field. Sitting on its back was a local car dealer, Ernie von Schledorn. The elephant started circling the field, walking on the warning track in front of the bleachers, part of some pre-game promotion. As I watched, I saw the elephant take a huge crap on the warning track. Then I heard my boss yell at me to get a shovel and a wheel barrow and clean up after the elephant. Now I understood why all my co-workers had disappeared. I raced under the stands to where the equipment was kept. The whole crew was waiting and laughing. I had been set up. By the time I got back on the field, the elephant was halfway around the track and had left another three enormous piles of crap in his trail.

I went out there after it and shoveled the crap into the wheelbarrow. By the time the elephant had left the field, my wheelbarrow was full to overflowing and fans were giving me the business. A few of them even stood and gave me a standing ovation as I left the field. I really heard from the other members of the crew. They called out to me, saying things like, "Welcome to the big leagues!" and, "I bet you wish you never took this job," but the opposite was true. I couldn't have been happier; I'd finally made it to the majors.

Chapter 6

A few weeks after I started working with the Brewers, one of the grounds crew workers quit. The Brewers offered his hours to me, so I essentially became a full-time seasonal member of the crew, sometimes working sixteen to eighteen hours when there was a home game. My career as a major league groundskeeper was beginning. There was so much to learn. The rest of that season was a fantastic experience. I really enjoyed the camaraderie of the crew, the teamwork we showed and the pride we took in our jobs.

Most people think all a groundskeeper does is cut the grass. That's certainly part of it but, when I started out, I was just another member of the crew, and I had to do all sorts of work. We had to get the field ready before games—yes, cutting the grass, but also manicuring the infield skin, patching the mound and plate, watering every surface, repairing damaged areas, uncovering the infield, setting up the batting cage, the pitching screen, the Fungo net and turf protection around the cage, then prepping for the game, raking the dirt, and picking up debris, all the fine-tuning necessary to make the field perfect. And, during the game, we have to be available as needed to work on the mound or batter's box, or cover the field when it rains and then, over the course of the game, we come out at scheduled times to maintain the field.

The next time you get to a game early, just watch how many people are on the field who aren't players. There are usually close to a dozen members of the grounds crew and they hardly ever stop working. In that way, we're kind of like umpires. If you don't notice us, but just notice how nice the field looks, we're probably doing a good job.

Work doesn't end with the final pitch. After the game, there is more work to be done, prepping the infield skin, the mounds and plates, watering them to build a moisture base in the clay, and, depending on the weather, covering the infield and preparing for the game the following day. And, when the team is out of town, that's the time for even more intensive maintenance—replacing sod, testing the soil, watering, working on equipment, keeping everything clean and preparing for special events like concerts. Then there's all the work few people realize the grounds crew does but, around the ballpark, particularly when I started out, if there was any need for physical labor, we usually got drafted to do it. At that time, we were the grounds and maintenance crew. It's not like that now. We don't oversee general maintenance. Back then, however, crew members were considered jacks-of-all trades around the ballpark. If office furniture needed to be moved, a picture hung, equipment unloaded, or a vendor needed help, we would get the call to do whatever the front office needed done. The days can be long, and the work can be physically demanding, but it's a great job if you love baseball.

One thing you learn quickly is that you don't tell tales about the team out of school. Even though you don't have much direct contact with the players, you're around them all the time. It's like any other workplace; over time, you get to know a little about just about everyone. Some guys are nice as can be, smile, say hello, and chat a little, while others are sometimes not so nice. That's understandable. They have high-pressure jobs that require a lot of focus. And there are jerks in every profession. Baseball is no different. Sometimes a few players that fans love can be more challenging to be around, and a guy fans hate might be terrific. Anytime you get twenty-five people together, you have a wide variety of personalities. It's especially great when you get to see them all interacting with their families on the field, creating special memories. You can relate to just about anyone in those moments. But gossip isn't part of the job. You don't talk to the press unless your boss tells you to. You don't even tell stories to your friends. There's no way of knowing if it might leak out to the public. If the front office discovers that you're the one responsible for a story that proves embarrassing to the team or upsets a player and affects his performance, you'll be sending resumes to other teams asking for jobs. People ask me questions about the team all the time, assuming I have inside information. I don't like to be rude, and I don't mind saying good things about people, but I have to tell them it's not appropriate for me to say much. Ask me about the field and I can talk all day!

I was pleased that, physically, I was holding up well. Finally, I had gone through a year of school without being badly hurt. Even while working and going to school, I still had to maintain my physical therapy at Ohio State for an hour three times a week, riding a stationary bicycle and doing other exercises to maintain my strength and flexibility. My knee was never going to magically "get better," and never cause me trouble again—I knew that. But, if I kept working on it, I felt I could do just about anything. I got to the point where I had stopped wearing my brace all the time. Although, if it was raining or snowing, and there was a chance of slipping, I would err on the side of caution and put it on. I had several different custom-made braces. One was custom painted scarlet and gray, Ohio State's colors. It was even decorated with some buckeye leaf stickers, like those the football players earn during the season and wear on their helmets. Like almost every Ohio State student, I was a huge Buckeyes fan.

Working on the Brewer's grounds crew, I still had to be careful, of course, but I could bend my knee, crouch down, and even jog a little bit when I needed to hurry. The Brewers knew I had physical issues with my knee—it was hard to ignore those big scars—but I was able to do everything I needed to do and was under no real restrictions from my doctor. I just had to use common sense while working, and make sure I didn't put too much stress on my right knee and use both my legs when doing physical labor. I'm proud of the fact the Brewer's never told me I wasn't doing my share of work or had to modify my duties. I was one of the guys.

I still limped a little and it still bothered me when someone would make a wisecrack, usually someone I didn't know, or a fan that had too much to drink and thought he was being funny by pointing out the way I walked. But I just loved being on the field. There is just something about being at the ballpark, the way it sounds, the way it smells. I love the smell of freshly cut grass, even though, ironically, I'm allergic to it! The way a field looks in the morning, covered with dew, with no one around, or at night, when lights go off, it's magical. There's no place like it in the world, and no place I'd rather be.

By the time I got done every day, I would be exhausted, in a good way, because I was doing what I loved. I also gained confidence. I now knew that I could do the work, and that I could hold a full-time job even with all the problems with my knee, and with the anxiety I still felt everyday worrying about having a panic attack or flash-back. I was becoming pretty good at keeping those hidden. At the end of the summer, just before I returned to school, the Brewers let me know that I was welcome to come back when school ended the following spring.

I returned to Columbus, went back to work at the Country Club and resumed taking classes. Because I was almost doubling up on my course load, I was on pace to finish school in only two and half years. I may have fallen behind at the start, but I was catching up fast. In another year and a half, I planned to graduate. I was doing well at school too. I was keeping my grades up and earning scholarships to help offset the costs. I was actually the first student to concentrate in sports turf management at Ohio State. Everyone else was focusing on either golf course management or lawn care. I didn't realize it at the time, but I was at the beginning of a new wave of groundskeepers coming to the major leagues with a background in science, and with a degree combined with experience. Now that's almost mandatory for many jobs in the field. That didn't mean that the older guys I was working with didn't know what they were doing. They did. They had just learned their craft by trial and error, and by talking to other groundskeepers and sharing their experience and expertise, rather than by taking classes. Some of them were self-taught or had taken some courses and did know some of the science.

I had the best of both worlds. I learned the science of sports turf management at school, then was able to gain practical knowledge and wisdom from people far more experienced than I. While a book can teach you about a subject, you only learn about people and how to manage them by working on a crew. If I was ever to head my own crew, I knew I would need to be just as proficient with my people skills as I was with soil science. Running a grounds crew also means managing a large and diverse staff, and interacting with all sorts of people, from the fans and the front office, to the players, vendors, security, and special events staff. You can know everything there is to know about taking care of a field but, if you don't know how to treat people, you'll never be successful.

It was exciting to be back at school and back with Denise. And it was doubly exciting because, in 1986, the Red Sox were fighting for a place in the postseason for the first time since I was a kid. While I was also a Brewers fan and wanted the team to do well, I have to admit that, even while I was working in Milwaukee, the Red Sox had a special place in my heart and I really looked forward to the times when the Sox were in town. That summer in Milwaukee, I got to see the Red Sox several times and got to be ball boy down the left field line. I'd get to warm up with Jim Rice between innings because I had a good arm. Jim loved to throw knuckleballs and so did I.

Most of the time, I was working, so I rarely had time to watch much of the games, but it was still thrilling to see the Red Sox, behind Roger Clemens, Wade Boggs, and Jim Rice, surge into first place, win the pennant and make it to the World Series. Of course, we all know what happened then. I was in my Statistics class. The professor allowed me to wear headphones and listen and, when Mookie Wilson bounced a ball through Bill Buckner's legs that probably cost the team a championship, I yelled out loud, and then he made me turn it off. I took the loss to the Mets just as hard as every other Red Sox fan.

Late that winter, in February 1987, the All England Lawn Tennis Club in England contacted me and asked if I wanted to intern with them for the upcoming summer. That's where they hold the Wimbledon Championships. It was an exciting offer, and the idea of going to London was intriguing. But, even though Wimbledon is the best-known and most-storied tennis facility in the world, it was not Fenway Park. It wasn't even County Stadium. I was flattered, but I felt that I now had my foot in the door in the major leagues. Though I knew working at Wimbledon would be an incredible experience,

I didn't know if it would help me reach my goal of being a head groundskeeper in the majors. I turned the offer down.

Spring break was approaching, and I planned to visit my brother Chip in San Francisco. Before I left, I contacted Barney Barron, the head of the San Francisco city grounds department, to ask if he had five minutes to meet with me when I was there to talk about Candlestick Park. He said, "Why don't you meet me at Candlestick, so we can walk the field and talk at the same time?" I was thrilled by the offer and made arrangements to meet him. That five minutes lasted three hours. It was fascinating to learn about the different challenges he faced maintaining a field located right next to the ocean. Although it didn't snow in the winter, it was often cold and damp. Responsibility for the field was shared with local government, so there were actually two staffs that took care of the park. Civic workers were responsible for the warning track, outfield, and foul territory, while the Giant's grounds crew mowed the infield and worked the infield skin, the mound, and the batter's box.

I sent him a thank-you letter when I returned home the next week. A week later, he called and asked if I wanted to intern with the San Francisco Giants that summer. I couldn't believe it. I excitedly called Chip and he offered to let me stay with him to save money if I wanted to come out. I thought about it a lot and came to the decision that the opportunity to get more experience in Major League Baseball and make more friends in the groundskeeping community was too good to pass up. The more ways I could learn, the better it would be for my career. I enthusiastically called Mr. Barron and accepted his kind offer.

"I'm glad you called," he said. "Because, if you're interested, I also spoke with my friend and colleague with the city of Anaheim and he said he would like you to intern with them, too, if you want."

I couldn't say no.

That summer was awesome. In a matter of only a few months I worked for the Brewers and interned for a few weeks with both the Giants and Angels. In addition to preparing the field for baseball, I also helped prep the field for a Los Angeles Rams football game at Anaheim Stadium. But it wasn't all fun. I found driving on the west coast a real challenge. San Francisco was bad enough but, when I got to Anaheim, where I stayed on the couch of a friend, I discovered that the freeways were sometimes six and seven lanes wide. The first few times I got lost and it took me a couple of hours to drive to the ballpark. I learned so much, and not all of it about taking care of the baseball field. I remember one older man I worked with in San Francisco knew I wanted to, one day, be heads groundskeeper, and I remember him telling me, "David, when you get to be in my position, I wouldn't recommend you hire your friends. You know, it's one thing to become friends with people at work, to earn their respect, but it's another thing when you hire a friend. You have to be their boss, but they think of you as a friend and they don't always understand the difference. Sometimes you have to make hard decisions." I never forgot that. I have been very fortunate that so many people have gone out of their way to give me advice and share their wisdom.

It was another exciting season on the field as well. When I was working for the Giants, the team was in first place heading toward the playoffs. When the Giants weren't playing well, they rarely drew big crowds to Candlestick, which was practically on the water at the edge of the city, hard to get to and often windy and cold. When they were winning, the ballpark was much livelier. That always makes it more exciting, even though it can mean more work. There's nothing quite like the buzz around a winning team. It's infectious, and that filters down to those of us who work at the ballpark.

Late that summer, Al Rosen, the former Cleveland third baseman who was the Giants general manager, called me into his office.

He'd been in baseball for years and I'd been hearing about him and reading about him since I was a kid—first as a player and then as a baseball executive with several teams. I had no idea why he wanted to talk with me and thought that, with Giants fighting for the pennant, he must have far more important things to do than meet with an intern. I thought that I must be in big trouble. When I went up to his office, I was almost trembling. I thought to myself, "Gosh, what did I do wrong?" As it turns out, I hadn't done anything wrong. In fact, it was quite the opposite. I guess I must have been doing a lot of things right. I was working hard, and I had been spending as much time as possible at the ballpark, focusing on the work and trying to ignore the flashbacks and all my other issues, trying to work them away. I was surprised when he offered me a full-time, salaried position with the Giants ground crew. In addition to my work ethic, the Giants appreciated my background in turf science. I wouldn't be the chief groundskeeper, but something like second assistant to the groundskeeper. All I had to do was say yes and my dream of having a permanent job in the major leagues would come true. There was just one problem. I still had several courses to complete before I earned my degree at Ohio State. My first thought was, "If I take this job, I don't know how I'll ever get my degree." I'd worked so hard that I didn't want to stop so close to finishing. There were no online courses or alternate ways to complete a degree back then. Then again, I also thought, "If I turn this down, I may never get another chance to have a full-time job in the major leagues." I felt like a kid who'd been drafted by a major league team out of high school, trying to decide whether to become a professional or accept a college scholarship. I thanked Mr. Rosen for the offer and told him I would have to think about it.

I walked out his office to a pay phone on one of the ramps leading into the stadium. I called my mother, then Denise, Chip, and Terry.

I had to talk this out with the four most important people in my life, all of whom I trusted and knew would understand my quandary. This was August, and we were already planning to celebrate my graduation in December with a trip to Cancun and Cozumel in Mexico. I had planned it that way, so I could send out resumes in the fall and, hopefully, have a job in the majors by the time the season started that spring. But I also had something else in mind. Denise was coming with us and I planned on asking her to marry me.

Now I didn't know what to do. If I accepted the job, I'd have to cancel the trip. I wasn't sure if Denise would like living in San Francisco. Heck, I didn't even know if she would say yes. Like me, she is a small-town girl. San Francisco is beautiful, but I also knew it was a very expensive place to live. Although the Giants offer was for a full-time job, I didn't know if I could afford to support the both of us on an entry-level salary. A million thoughts were going through my head.

They were all good listeners. After talking it out and wrestling with my decision for a few days, I went back to see Mr. Rosen. I thanked him for the offer and told him that I was humbled, but I felt that I should go back to school and finish my degree. He completely understood, and I left the Giants on good terms at the end of my internship. I returned to Ohio and, that fall, I sent out resumes to every major league team and to many other potential employers in the turf industry as well. Despite my experience, I knew that getting a big-league job was no certainty.

I was thrilled with the response. Even before graduation, I received a couple of job offers. One was from Scott's, the lawn care company and one of the leaders in the field. The other was from the Brewers. There was no question which one I would accept. The Brewers were the only major league team to offer me a job. In fact, they created a new position just for me. Even though the salary was ten or twelve thousand dollars less than the offer from Scott's, I knew I couldn't turn it down. I'd already turned down one big league job. If I did so again, I might never have another chance.

In December, the trip to Mexico was everything I hoped for. And Denise said yes! Though not right away. It was kind of funny. For the past couple of years, I think everyone assumed we would get married, and Denise would sort of joke about it every once in a while, asking me, "So, David, will you marry me?"

Every time she did, I would just laugh and say, "What? Oh, that's the question I'm supposed to ask." I never thought she was serious. It became a kind of routine; she'd ask, and I would always answer the same way: "What?" By the time we got to Mexico, everyone in my family knew that I was going to ask her. I had it all planned out. I wanted it to be very romantic. In my mind, it always ended the same: I would ask her, she would say yes, and we would embrace and begin our lives together.

At the end of a beautiful day, I asked her to take a walk with me. We strolled along the beach at sunset, the Gulf of Mexico lapping at our feet, the sky changing from blue and gold to pink. We stood together and looked at the sun as it dipped into the waters at the edge of the horizon.

"Denise," I said, making sure my voice didn't crack with emotion. "Will you marry me?" This was the moment I had been waiting for.

"What?"

I couldn't believe it. Didn't she hear me? How could she not have heard me? Is she stalling so she can say no? It seemed to be the longest pause I'd ever experienced.

"Is that THE question?" she said.

Then she started laughing and teasing me. When she said "What?" the first time, she was turning the tables on me. Turns out that all those times she'd been asking me, she was serious. And, oh yeah, she said "Yes."

That's Denise for you, always able to put a smile on my face. Despite all the trying times, she has helped me through every situation and never wavered. I could not ask for a better partner, or a better mother for our girls.

We all had a wonderful time and, even though I was still tortured by nightmares every night, even on vacation, my health issues seemed to be mostly in the past. Although I was still dealing with physical and emotional pain, with a college degree, a wedding to plan, and a job starting soon, I was looking forward to the rest of my life. I felt as if I had finally succeeded. I was graduating from college just a few months later than most of my friends and was ready to live a normal life.

I quickly learned to take nothing for granted. Before going on vacation, I had heard horror stories from people who had gone to Mexico and gotten sick from eating street food, or from the water, so I was careful the whole time we were there. I was so worried ahead of time that I even went to see my doctor. He gave me a prescription in case I got sick while I was there, and he told me to be careful of what I ate and drank. I was, but I still ate a great deal of red meat and fatty foods. Fortunately, none of us got sick.

On the flight back to Chicago, however, we were given the option of steak or chicken meals. Because I pigged out on vacation, I decided to eat the chicken, thinking it was healthier than the steak. What a mistake! About an hour into the drive home to Ohio I started feeling sick. I broke out in a heavy sweat from a high fever and my stomach started cramping. I got ill so quickly that my mother checked us into a hotel somewhere along the road. I barely made it inside before throwing up. The next thing I remember, I woke in a hospital with an IV in my arm. Three days had passed. It was a good thing we had stopped. I had become severely dehydrated from Salmonella food poisoning. On top of that, I had a bacterial infection known as Shigella that is one of the causes of dysentery. To top it off, I had picked up an intestinal parasite! The doctor thought it was all likely due to the chicken I ate on the plane, although it was impossible to say for certain. All I know is that I was the only one in our family to become ill.

My recovery from food poisoning took two long weeks. I had to delay starting the job in Milwaukee until I regained my strength. Even then, it was another five months before my body was free of the parasite and I felt completely healthy again. I knew getting to the big leagues would be tough, but this seemed a little much!

Even though it was winter, we still had to start preparing the field, which always took a beating from the games the Packers played. The winters are cold in Wisconsin and last a long time, so we had to take advantage of every break in the weather to get the field ready for the season opener in April.

One day in May, my boss approached me and told me I had to go see his boss, one of the team's vice presidents. I asked what was going on and he said, "He's pretty pissed. You need to go up there right now!" I couldn't imagine what I had done. When I got to his office, it was clear that he was angry. He ordered me to sit down and started cursing me out.

"This is a bunch of BS. I don't know what you think you were doing but, after we went out of our way to create a position for you, and hire you, and hold the job when you got sick, how dare you turn around and start sending out resumes already?! That's a bunch of BS!"

I was stunned. I had no idea what he was talking about. "I didn't send out any resumes," I stammered.

He looked at me skeptically. "Well, then," he said, almost yelling, "Why would George Steinbrenner call up Mr. Selig and tell him he wanted to offer you the Yankees head groundskeeper position if you didn't send him your resume?"

Apparently, the owner of the New York Yankees had called the Brewer's owner, Mr. Selig, as a courtesy to ask permission to talk to me. Most major league teams generally don't try to hire anyone from the staff of another team without clearing it at the top. The Yankees wanted me to come to New York for an interview but, apparently, the job was mine for the taking.

My head started to spin. It was exciting news, but I couldn't figure out how it had happened. I hadn't sent out any resumes since October. The Yankees must have sat on it, finally made a decision, and then learned I was with the Brewers.

"Gosh," I said, "I sent the Yankees a resume way back in October. I sent a resume to almost every major league team back then, but I haven't sent any since I was hired."

The VP still didn't believe me. "Let me tell you something," he said, "if you go to New York for an interview and they offer you the job, you better take it. Because, either way, if you go down there for an interview, you are not welcome back here, even if you turn it down."

I hardly knew what to think, I was almost shaking. I hadn't even been thinking of leaving, but here was a major league team, not just offering me a job, but offering me the top spot.

As a Red Sox fan, could I really work for the Yankees? Did I want to live in the big city? Milwaukee still seemed like a pretty big place to me. There was also the idea of working for George Steinbrenner. Everyone knew he was incredibly demanding and difficult to work for. It seemed like he hired and fired managers every other week. Still, I was intrigued, and honored Mr. Steinbrenner had called. I was actually more familiar with him than the Brewer's knew. My uncle had worked for a shipping company in Cleveland, where Steinbrenner was from, and his father had operated the Kinsman Marine Transit Company, another shipping firm. George's father and my uncle were friends, and sometimes visited together. The offer was tempting. Here I was, only a few months out of college, and I was already being offered a job with one of the biggest teams in baseball, to take care of one of the most famous ballparks in all of baseball, Yankee Stadium.

Apart from all my other concerns, though, was that I wondered if I was ready for a job with so much responsibility. I already knew that being a head groundskeeper was demanding. Apart from the actual work on the field, I'd have to manage a budget, be in charge of a staff, and be the new guy coming in and taking over for staff that had probably been in place for years. What if it didn't work out? What if I wasn't ready and failed? I felt like the rookie who'd just been called up to the big leagues that hadn't even unpacked and was now being asked to pitch the first game of the World Series. There was even more to it than that. I was engaged to Denise, but she was living in Ohio. I was still having nightmares every night, the amount of which ebbed and flowed, depending on how busy I was. And Denise, who I was about to marry, knew nothing about them. In my mind, I was already rehearsing how I would tell her, but I really had no idea how to explain my symptoms. I didn't understand them. How could someone else?

I thanked the Yankees for the opportunity, but I declined the interview and decided to stay in Milwaukee. Besides, maybe the Red Sox would give me a call someday. Now that I had reached the big leagues, that was my real dream.

Chapter 7

*V*ictims of PTSD react to the disorder in a variety of ways. Some lash out to keep people away and to avoid confronting their issues. Others hide, staying inside their homes with the shades drawn or living in remote areas. An astonishing number of PTSD victims withdraw so much that they become homeless. Some try to medicate their troubles with alcohol or drugs or sex. Addictive behaviors serve as a shield and keep victims from finding out what is wrong and seeking treatment. Until a PTSD victim gets treatment and embarks on the road to recovery, each finds their own way to cope with what is often an overwhelming illness that affects them each and every moment of their lives.

I worked. And worked. And worked.

I was in the major leagues, but still hadn't fulfilled my goal of becoming head groundskeeper. I wanted to make sure that, if I ever did get another offer, I was absolutely prepared for it. In a sense, I was like a ballplayer making sure I had all the fundamentals down, perfecting my craft so that, when the big opportunity arrived, I would be ready. The worst thing would be to accept a big job and screw it up. I knew that could end my career.

So I worked. Over the next three years, I remained in the same position, the second assistant to the groundskeeper. I worked as hard as I could, not only learning how to put into practice what I had learned in the classroom, but learning how to be a leader and a manager, to teach our staff, learn from others more experienced, and get along with everyone at the ballpark, from the club president and field manager to the part-time seasonal workers we hired in the summer.

I found it easy to justify working all the time, even though I now realize I was fooling myself. Back then, I was at the beginning of my career and I told myself that everything I was doing was for the future, that eventually I would earn a bigger salary and have a more prestigious position and that would benefit my family. That first year, Denise was still in Ohio, making plans for the wedding, so it wasn't like I had many distractions. And there was a lot of work to do. In 1988, County Stadium was used to film scenes for the movie "Major League," starring Charlie Sheen. Much of their filming was done at night, so, some days, I would come in at noon and not leave until the next morning. There were times I would stay at the ballpark for twelve, fourteen, even sixteen hours. I didn't know what else to do.

Denise still didn't know what was going on inside me. Almost every day, while driving home from work, I would practice what to say, speaking out loud to myself, telling her about how messed up I felt I was, about the attacks of panic and anxiety I would feel when I heard the squeal of tires or heard an engine race. But, when I saw her, I would just freeze and not say anything. It didn't get any better after we were married that November. In the days before the wedding, I was nervous, like any groom, except I was also nervous about talking to her—I felt I had to do that before we got married. But I didn't. Even after the wedding, when we moved in to our first home in Milwaukee, I still couldn't talk to her about it, not even the nightmares. Of course, she knew I had trouble sleeping—I kept the TV on, after all, and would wake up with a start several times a night. I know it sounds crazy, and I realize now that it was, but I didn't bring it up, and neither did she. It was there, but we didn't acknowledge it. It's funny how your mind works when you're avoiding something.

My knee gave me the perfect excuse not to talk, to let Denise believe that my knee was the reason I was sometimes distant or short-tempered. I was usually feeling some physical pain, at certain times more than others, depending on what I was doing, but the pain never went away and, over time, began to increase. Doctors had done just about all they could at the time for my knee. It was functional but didn't work the way a knee was designed to work. Periodically, scar tissue would build up. Due to the accident, the subsequent surgeries, the way my hamstring had been used to make up for my torn ligaments, and the surgical staples, stresses were placed on my knee and the surrounding bone and tissue in ways the joint wasn't meant to bear. In combination, the physical and emotional pain was completely exhausting.

Overworking was a choice I sometimes made. It was better for me to stay busy than be idle because, if I had the time, I'd think about my knee pain or worry about my other symptoms. That's one of the things about PTSD that impacts so many victims: We don't let people get too close. Many victims who are married end up divorcing, pushing away the people they should be depending on and turning to. I was just so ashamed of feeling the way I did that I didn't want to confront those feelings, or even admit I had them. And that often meant spending time away from Denise, who I actually needed and depended on more than ever before. When times were bad, I would withdraw, but when I was feeling good, we had a great time. I just never quite knew when that was going to be.

It doesn't make much sense now but, at the time, that's how much PTSD was affecting my thinking. There were times I acted out and became angry, not because of anything Denise had done, but because I was feeling vulnerable, that she was getting too close to me and putting me in a position that was forcing me to confront my issues. I didn't want to do that, so I would say something cruel or thoughtless, give her the silent treatment, or stay at work when I didn't have to. I would feel terrible afterwards, but it was a way to protect myself, and I thought she would be better off if I was not there. I was more angry at myself than her and it caused me to lash out.

I'm incredibly fortunate Denise didn't divorce me. I can't imagine how hard it must have been for her to have a husband who wasn't home and who was barely there emotionally. What must have seemed like a small issue when we were dating was much more pronounced now that we were living together as husband and wife. But, when we were together, I was petrified I wouldn't say the right thing, that I wouldn't act the right way, or I'd have a mood swing and say something I didn't mean. So it was just easier to stay away, to volunteer to do extra work, or just find an excuse to stay at the ballpark for another hour or two.

I had the reputation of not just being a hard worker but being a guy who joked around and was easy to get along with. I was but, many times, that was just a mask too, a way to keep people away, to keep from confronting my real feelings. I wasn't healing in any way, and overwork wasn't helping my knee either. The knee cap began to deteriorate and soften, a condition known as chondromalacia. The meniscus, the cartilage in the knee that provides cushioning, was wearing thin and tearing. It seemed like every six months or a year, I would have to have surgery of some kind to try to repair the damage. The operations weren't as severe as my earlier surgeries. I tried to laugh them off by referring to them as "tune-ups," but no surgery is ever something you can laugh off, and I would have to undergo physical therapy after each one. Most of the time, my knee would work better for a while—or at least the deterioration would slow—but the pain never went away. It just got worse.

On its own, chronic pain can be just as devastating as PTSD. Today, there are pain clinics and pain is often treated as something on its own, apart from the cause. But, back then, pain was generally considered a byproduct of the underlying medical issues. Apart from some pain medication immediately after surgery, I wasn't on prescription pain medication all the time because I didn't like dealing with the side effects. I just tried to live with it, to suck it up and keep going.

That's not to say that every moment of life was terrible, or that I didn't enjoy working for the Brewers. I did. When I was hired, it was with the understanding that, when the head groundskeeper Harry Gill retired in three years, his assistant, Gary VandenBerg, would replace him and I would become his first assistant. Sadly, Harry passed away before he could retire. In only my third season, I became Gary's first assistant and he and Gabe Paul Jr., the VP of Stadium Operations, and Mr. Selig, the team owner, couldn't have been nicer to me. Gary gave me a great deal of responsibility and authority and made me feel as if I were a co-director. That's not something many other people would have done. It was a sad day for me when he passed away in 2011 after a long bout with cancer. He wasn't just a boss, but a dear friend and a brother.

Major league groundskeepers often share information with one another, so if you're successful it doesn't take very long for others in the field to hear about it. Today, major league groundskeepers get together once each year for an annual meeting where we have meetings and seminars. That all kind of started when I was in Milwaukee. The Toro Company and Turface Athletics, a company that makes infield conditioners, started sending MLB groundskeepers to the annual meeting of the Golf Course Superintendents Association of America. Every other team just sent the head groundskeeper, but Gary and the Brewers always sent me as well, so I quickly got to know almost everyone in the field.

In 1989, Denise became pregnant with our first daughter. It was a difficult pregnancy and she had to make sure she didn't over-extend herself. At the same time, Ohio State University decided to remove the artificial surface in the football stadium, known to fans as "the Horseshoe" due to its shape, and replace it with a grass field. It's hard to believe today that artificial fields were once in so many ballparks and stadiums, particularly when you consider how terrible they were to play on and how bad they looked. But, thirty-five or forty years ago, when many of those fields were installed, teams didn't realize how much upkeep they required and how bad the hard surface could be for the physical health of the athletes. Today, it's come around almost full circle. Technological advances in turf management result in natural grass fields that are much more resilient and provide a better surface for most sports. Even today's artificial turf has improved, offering much better cushioning and "truer" response. The first artificial fields were little more than the kind of fake plastic grass you see today on doormats, placed on top of a thin pad on asphalt over concrete. It took a toll on athletes in terms of injuries. Many players didn't like it. As the slugger Richie Allen once said, "If a horse won't eat it, I don't want to play on it." Today, with payrolls in the hundreds of millions of dollars, teams are much more concerned with making certain the playing surface is safe. That's my number one job—something I take a lot of pride in. Aesthetics are important, sure, but not as important as safety and playability. One mistake can cost a team a game, and maybe a pennant, or destroy a player's career. I know what that feels like.

Ohio State contacted me and asked if I wanted to be in charge of the changeover and be responsible for the upkeep of not just the Horseshoe, but all their athletic fields. They made it clear that they wanted me and said I had the right of first refusal. It was a tempting offer. With our first child on the way, Denise and I would be back near home, where our child could grow up around family. I had lived in Columbus during college and we were both comfortable with the city. We had our favorite hangouts and restaurants and still had many friends there. But the health of Denise and our baby were most important. Her doctor believed a move at that time would be risky for the pregnancy. I told Ohio State that I appreciated the offer and was honored they had asked, but that we would stay in Milwaukee. Our first daughter, Cacky, was born a short time later, in the summer of 1990. Her given name is Catherine, after my aunt, who I always called Cacky.

As a new father, I was thrilled, but it was also the middle of baseball season and I my work pace didn't slow, I was still at the ballpark all the time. That fall, I was catching a ride home with my boss, Gary, after we worked a Packers home game in Milwaukee. I felt fine when we left County Stadium but, about halfway home, while Gary and I were chatting, I felt a wave of vertigo wash over me and began to feel extremely ill. One minute we were talking and, the next thing I knew, my head was throbbing. The faintest light hurt my eyes and I was nauseous. When I got home, I could barely walk. I staggered through the door like a drunk. I went to bed but suffered an awful night. By morning, I could barely stand up or even lift my head without exerting a tremendous amount of effort.

Denise insisted that I go see the doctor, and I didn't resist. After only a few minutes, he told me he suspected that I had viral meningitis and sent me to the emergency room. Meningitis is contagious, so when I got to the hospital they isolated me right way. As a nurse took my vital signs, an intern told me he had to take a spinal tap to confirm the diagnosis. He told me to lie on my side and curl into a ball to open space between the vertebrae. As soon as he stuck the needle in, my left leg and arm spasmed as if I were being electrocuted. It was the intern's first spinal tap and he had struck a nerve. He tried again and, this time, was able to extract some fluid. Doctors confirmed that I had meningitis. I was quarantined in the hospital for a week. Our daughter was only five months old and I was still contagious, so Denise wasn't allowed to visit. After a week in the hospital, I went home but, for a while, I had to wear a mask to protect the baby. Incredibly, a few months later, I contracted viral meningitis again. It may have been PTSD-related. Today, doctors know that the symptoms of PTSD can negatively affect your immune system. Many PTSD patients have increased levels of inflammation and researchers believe that triggers changes in cells in the immune system. That's not uncommon. We're in a state of anxiety and panic so much that the body's immune system just kind of short-circuits. The constant state of vigilance I maintained to keep control over my panic attacks, combined with exhaustion from overworking simply wore me out, and that may have left my system too weak to defend itself. That may have played a role in both my initial illness and the relapse.

A few years later, our second daughter was born. My PTSD symptoms had not improved. In fact, as time went on, they were slowly getting worse. I would become moody and sometimes turn little problems into big ones, lose my patience and say things I didn't mean. Then I'd realize what I had done or said and be overwhelmed by guilt, something I deeply regret because I really wanted to be the best father and husband I could be. It was an emotional rollercoaster for Denise and the girls. One minute, I'd be fine and, the next, I'd become quiet and withdrawn and start to brood, then flip back and be apologetic. Denise and the girls never knew how I would react. It was particularly bad around the anniversaries of the traumatic events, including my dad's death. Denise and the girls walked on eggshells. I was never physically violent, but I'm sure there were times that my anger was frightening to them. When times were good, they were very good, but when they were bad, they were awful. In the end, I became more and more withdrawn, and I beat myself up for it. To this day, the fact that I wasn't a better husband and father is the biggest regret of my life. I hope others don't wait as long as I did to get help.

Still, with two children, Milwaukee was feeling like home. But, as time passed, my profile as a groundskeeper was increased and I received more offers to become head groundskeeper elsewhere. In 1993, I received a particularly big boost, and I have Paul McCartney to thank for that. In the middle of the season, McCartney played a concert at County Stadium. To accommodate the crowd, an enormous stage facing toward home plate was built across the outfield, and temporary seats were installed on the field between the stage and the stands. It was a huge undertaking. The Brewers were on the road, and we had a small window in which to work—the stage and seating would have to go up, come down, and the field returned to normal. All the temporary infrastructure was designed with this in mind. The affected part of the field in front of the stage was a twenty-four-foot wide road for forklifts, which we covered with over two hundred sheets of plywood. The seating area in front of the stage was covered with a special felt pad and mat to protect the grass, not only from the staging, but from the thousands of people jumping and dancing to McCartney's music. It was a challenge, but we knew how to protect the field. Unfortunately, it poured rain almost the entire time—during setup, during the show, and while it was being torn down. As a result, after everything was removed, you could tell something other than baseball had taken place on the grass. The ground had softened and much of the outfield was marked in an enormous grid-like pattern. One spot where the forklifts had done the bulk of their driving was particularly bad. Lucky for us, the actual field hadn't been damaged too badly and we knew how to make that playable fairly quickly. We aerated it, top-dressed it with green calcine clay, which firmed it up, and spread grass clippings to try to hide the damage, but it still looked awful. And the Yankees were coming into town, which meant lots of media and lots of attention. What to do?

Gary and I put our heads together. There wasn't really anything we could do to remove the grid-like pattern, so we decided to mask it. I drew up a design, and Gary and I consulted with Gabe Paul Jr., to make sure it was okay. Then I worked all night. Periodically, I would go up into the stands to make sure it looked right. In the morning, I couldn't wait to show them. You've probably noticed this with your own lawn but, depending on the way you cut it and the way the grass lays, it creates a pattern. Working with Gary, we decided to use this to our advantage. We created a pleasing geometric design for the field and, by using a golf greens mower— which have a roller—were able to create a very distinctive pattern that made the grid marks in the outfield virtually unnoticeable. In that way, we drew everyone's attention toward the infield. The Yankees came to town and all announcer Phil Rizzuto could talk about was how great the field looked—and, on television, it looked even better than in person. The announcers couldn't stop talking about it. Afterwards, we received hundreds of letters from fans asking how we created the pattern, and many, many inquiries from other turf management professionals. It was incredibly gratifying for Gary and me to see the hard work of our crew so widely recognized. Eventually, I would even write books about how to take care of your lawn and use some of the same methods to make similar designs in your own yard. I describe this in some detail in my books *Picture Perfect: Mowing Techniques for Lawns, Landscapes and Sports* and *The Lawn Bible: How to Keep in Green, Groomed, and Growing Every Season of the Year.*

During those early years in Milwaukee, I probably ended up turning down eight or ten other jobs. Some were easy to say no to, but others—like the Ohio State job—were not. At various times the Yankees, Royals, Giants, Cardinals, Indians, Dodgers, Twins, and Mariners all either made an inquiry, offered me a job, or had me in for interviews. I was sincerely appreciative of all of them. Some offers were tempting, but just weren't right for my family. Of course, I was hoping to get a call from the Red Sox. I was friendly with their groundskeeper, Joe Mooney, but he showed no signs of retiring. The only job I applied for was with the Rockies, who were preparing to move into a new stadium in 1995. I still had fond memories of my short time in Colorado as a ranch hand, my brother Chip still lived in Denver, and I thought it would be a great place to raise a family. There were many applicants, and it eventually came down to two of us—me and the Oakland A's groundskeeper, my friend Mark. He was their first choice, but it turned out that he was under contract. So I got a call from the Rockies on a Friday and they asked me, "If we make you an offer on Monday, will you accept it?"

I said "Yes." Over the weekend, however, they ended up working out a deal with Oakland. Mark was able to get out of his contract and take the position. Well, now the A's had an opening.

They said to the Rockies, "Hey, you just went through this interview process. Who do you think is the best person for us to talk to?" The Rockies said they should hire me.

Billy Beane, Oakland's general manager, a former player who was later made famous for his work in the bestselling book "Moneyball," flew me out twice for interviews. He is one of the nicest guys I've ever met in the game. What really impressed me was how much he talked about family and how important it was to him. After the second interview, I was offered the job and given a few days to think it over. I came back to Milwaukee and gave a talk at an inner-city school in Milwaukee with the Brewer's general manager at the time, former Oakland third baseman Sal Bando. As we were riding back to the ballpark, we started talking.

"David, are you going to take that job with the A's?" he asked me.

"You know, Sal, I'm incredibly honored and flattered and humbled by their interest and Billy couldn't have been nicer, but I just don't think it's the right move for my family. The park is in kind of a tough neighborhood, and I want Denise to be able to come down with the girls to the park and not have to worry what might happen if she makes a wrong turn. And cost of living out there's a lot more than Milwaukee. I'm just not sure it's the right move."

"You know, David," he said, "you can always find another job; you can't find another family."

I'll never forget that. That was exactly how I felt. The next morning, I thanked Billy for the opportunity and respectfully declined the A's offer. He completely understood. (In a funny twist, about a decade later, Billy was offered the job of GM for the Red Sox. He turned it down after initially saying yes because he had divorced and wanted to stay in California to be near his daughter.)

This was August of 1994. The baseball players had just gone on strike. Strikes had happened before and been resolved relatively quickly. About a half hour after hanging up the phone with Billy, one of my co-workers came up to me.

"Are you going to the eleven o'clock meeting, or are you going to the one o'clock meeting?" he asked.

I said, "I don't know what you're talking about," I said.

"There are two meetings today," he said. "One at eleven and another at one. The rumor is that everybody going to the eleven o'clock meeting is getting laid off because of the strike."

I went straight to Gary.

"What the hell's going on?" I asked him. "I just turned down a job with the A's. Am I getting laid off?"

He said he wasn't sure, but he didn't think so, and suggested I go see Gabe Paul Jr.

"Gabe, I just turned down this job with Billy Bean, like, a half hour ago. Am I getting laid off? Should I call him back?"

"No," he said. "We'd love for you to stay."

That was a great relief, but a lot of my friends were laid off, which was tough for me to see. They had a hard time over the next few months. I felt for them and their families. I think the front office staff went from something like eighty-six to about forty, and those of us who did stay filled in wherever needed, even taking over the switchboard and answering the phones. It was tough, because the strike didn't end until the following season, lasting 232 days. Except for a few football games and other events, we had to keep the field ready for a game that wasn't going to be played.

As I said before, when times were good, they were very good. As the girls got older, they were able to come to the ballpark. The Brewers were family friendly and, when they were old enough, the girls sometimes joined me on the field. I can't thank Mr. Selig and Gabe and Gary enough for that opportunity. Denise made little grounds crew uniform shirts for each of them. They had their own little wheelbarrows and sprinkling cans and rakes and trowels. We had a lot of fun as they "helped me" prepare the field, collecting baseballs after batting practice, and then working around home plate. By then, fans would be filling the stands and they often left the field to cheers and ovations from the folks in the box seats. They were more popular than I was, that's for sure!

We were becoming part of the community and, as the girls got older and we made friends, more and more people became aware that I was a groundskeeper. And, when you are a groundskeeper, everyone expects your yard to be perfect. And, for a while, mine was. It was always perfectly manicured, not a blade of grass out of place, smooth as a pool table. We had a flower garden that included some wildflowers, and Cacky loved to pick little bouquets for Denise and me. One day while picking flowers, she spotted some dandelions where the edge of the driveway and the yard met. They were weeds to me but, to her, they were gorgeous. She bent down and looked at the flower heads closely, then picked them up and showed me. She said "Daddy, look how pretty these yellow flowers are up close. They have pretty little curly things in the flower." I'd never noticed, and I left the few remaining dandelions alone, so she could enjoy them. About a week later, they had turned to seed. She asked, "What are they now?" I explained that they were seeds and showed how they floated off when you blew on them. The next thing I know, she was picking them, and we were chasing each other around the yard blowing dandelion seeds all over the place. She called them "blow flowers" and we would also scour the ground for four-leaf clovers and makes chains of them. I realized that my war against the weeds, which are just undesirable plants out of place, was over. If a few dandelions and weeds made her happy....

Later, when she was in preschool, she had a birthday party and invited the whole class. One after another, parents drove up the drive and dropped off their children and I stood outside to greet them and show them the way to the party. I came back out and noticed one mother dropping off a child all by herself. I thought I'd seen her husband when they first pulled in. I said hello and said, "Isn't your husband here with you?"

"Yes, he is here," she said.

"Where is he? I answered, "I'd like to say hello."

"He is walking around your yard to see if he can find a weed!"

I laughed out loud and couldn't believe he was actually doing that. "I could have saved him a trip," and then told her about all the dandelions.

Unfortunately, there are not as many happy memories with the girls as there should be. I was at the ballpark so much that, in many ways, I left Denise to take care of them alone. I was ashamed of that but, instead of spending less time at the ballpark, I would spend even more time there, so I wouldn't have to confront my feelings.

One time, Denise was running an errand with the girls and drove by the ballpark. The girls recognized it, and Cacky said to her sister, "Oh, look. That's where Daddy lives." I was crushed when Denise told me that. Even today, thinking about that brings tears to my eyes.

Chapter 8

The 1995 baseball season was exciting. The Brewers didn't do well, but the Red Sox made it to the postseason for the first time in almost a decade and their dynamic, slugging first baseman, Mo Vaughn, was named American League MVP. Although they didn't make it to the World Series, where the Braves eventually topped the Indians, I was looking forward to my childhood team giving me something to root for over the next several seasons.

That October, after the season ended, we were given permission to re-sod the field. That entails a great deal of work. All of the old sod is removed while the remaining soil gets reconditioned and graded. Then new sod is installed and treated with TLC as it takes root. Today, we don't even use soil. Instead, a sand-based or modified sand-based root zone is used. At County Stadium, there were offices and storage rooms in the area under the outfield bleachers. During the offseason, office personnel, delivery trucks, and people working in grounds and maintenance would often park just outside, in a concourse area reserved for pedestrians during games. During games, a large gate was kept closed to prevent vehicles from entering the area, but during the off-season, that was left open. Access was controlled by a security guard who manned a guard shack and operated a single arm gate. It was easier than opening and closing the bigger gate. He was mostly there just to control access, give directions, tell visitors where to park and where to find whoever they were looking for. Otherwise, the area was wide open. Anyone could drive through the parking lot right up to the guard shack.

On October 24 I wrote a memo to team employees asking everyone to please park in the normal parking lot the following day. We'd been conditioning the soil and re-grading the field and the sod was due to arrive the following day. To accommodate that, we needed to open an outfield gate, so forklifts and other heavy equipment could enter the park. I didn't want to worry about a parked car being in the way or being damaged. Everyone understood.

October 25th was one of those picture-perfect Indian summer days—a little crisp in the morning, sunny, clear air, the leaves still changing on the trees. By late morning, the temperature had warmed to the mid-seventies. Perfect weather for working outside and ideal conditions for laying new sod. It was a great day. With the old sod removed, you could smell the earth.

At the left field end of the bleachers, there was break in the stands and a double-field gate that allowed vehicles access to the field whenever we had the need. During the Paul McCartney concert, for example, most of the staging had entered through that gate. We opened it wide earlier that morning and left it open, so the sod could be delivered.

Just before noon, I was out in left field, raking around an irrigation head, making sure it was exposed but didn't stick up too much, when I heard an automobile. As I've said, I was hypervigilant about car noises, so I picked up on this right away. I knew there was not supposed to be a car near the bleachers, and this one sounded like it was going fast.

I looked up and saw a car coming around the bleachers, then accelerating as it turned toward the open gate to the field. I threw down my rake and ran toward the gate, my hands waving in the air, yelling to get the driver's attention.

"Whoa, whoa. Stop!! STOP!!" A car driving onto the field would destroy all our hard work and set the project back.

By then, the car was about forty feet away. All I could see was a woman's face behind the windshield, an enormous smile on her face. She seemed to register that I was in her path, but instead of braking the car, she floored it, driving right through the gate, and right toward me. In an instant, I was back at McDonald's in 1981. The memories flooded in like no time had passed. I felt a shiver run up my spine and the hair stand up on the back of my neck and arms and legs. I knew she was going to run me down.

I wanted to run away, but I was frozen. She was coming at me too fast. Instinctively, I turned, just as I had in 1981, raised my left leg and held my arms out, as if I could somehow stiff-arm the car away. The next thing I knew, I was in the air, crashing into the windshield then rolling off the driver's side, landing heavily in a pile on the warning track near the wall, just inside the gate.

I couldn't wrap my head around what had just happened. It did not seem real, yet here I was, on the ground and the car that just struck me was speeding off tearing down the warning track as if it were a race track, flying toward home plate. When she rounded the track in front of the backstop, she fish-tailed and threw an enormous rooster-tail plume of dirt into the stands as her tires spun in the crushed granite surface.

The other two grounds keepers on the field were starting to react. One raced over to me, asking if I was okay and what to do. I couldn't even tell if I was hurt yet. I told him, "Lock up the gates behind the bleachers so she can't get away and call 911!"

I was still on the ground, still in shock, trying to comprehend what was happening. I watched the car continue to circle the field. She raced up the warning track off the first baseline, hung a left as she approached the outfield wall, and accelerated again. I was stunned. She aimed her car right at me. It seemed as if I was her target, as if she had come to the ballpark determined to run me down until I was dead. It was unreal. She was coming straight toward me. This time, I was afraid I would be run over. I tried to roll over and turn, to press my body up against the padding of the outfield wall, making myself as small a target as possible. As she raced closer, I thought to myself, "Holy shit, she's gonna hit me again," and braced for the impact. It was almost as if I was in the corner of that entranceway to McDonald's again. Then, at the last second, she swerved away and slammed on the brakes, missing me by only a few feet. I looked up, in absolute fear for my life. I had no idea what was taking place. Did she have a gun? Would she back up and take aim at me again?

I looked at her as she leaned up over from the driver's seat toward the passengers' window. She smiled and gave me a big wave.

What the hell was happening?

She stepped on the gas pedal and peeled out, throwing track material on me as she tore out the gate, off the field and toward the bleachers.

My heart felt as if it was going to explode. I was in a panic, half-frozen with fear, but also worried what she might do next. There were others all around the ballpark and, for all I knew, she might turn around and come back. Just like McDonald's and at physical therapy, this wasn't an incident that happened quickly and was then over. This was a nightmare that just kept going.

I grabbed onto the wall pad where it met the gate and pulled myself to my feet, thinking that I had to see where she went. I don't know how I managed to walk. It must have been the adrenaline, because, at this point, I knew I was hurt but I wasn't registering a lot of pain. I was focused on staying alive and keeping others from being hurt. I went through the gate and, just as I did, I could hear her SCREAMING at the lone security guard to let her out—the big gate was closed, and she was out of her car. The single arm, orange-and-white-striped gate was splintered on the ground. To gain access to the field, she had just driven right through it.

I could see her more clearly now. She was about forty, wearing a trench coat over a business suit, screaming at the top of her lungs, using every cuss word available, yelling at him to let her out, telling him to go to hell, asking "Don't you know who I am?" She was completely off the wall. Every few moments, she would stop, her eyes rolling back in her head as she looked up in the air and mumbled something. Then she'd snap out of it and start screaming. "Who the fuck do you think you are? Don't you know who I am???" My nerves were frayed. I felt like throwing up. Was I in the Twilight Zone?

Then I noticed that her car was still running. There was nothing to stop her from jumping back in and racing the field again or running down the guard or anyone else in her way, including me. I lurched over to the car, reached in and turned it off, pulling the keys from the ignition and taking them so she couldn't start it up again. Instantly, she stopped screaming at the guard and turned. As I got out of the car, she ran right up to me, inches from my face and started screaming at me, telling me to give her back the keys, cussing me out in every way imaginable—she didn't miss a word.

"I'm sorry, ma'am. I can't do that," I said, but it didn't help. She went around me, climbed in the car, slammed the door shut and kept screaming.

It had taken only a few minutes—but seemed like forever—before the county deputies arrived. I recognized the officers because they often provided security during games. They asked me what had happened, and I blurted out how she had run me down and driven all around the field. Now the deputies had to arrest her. She had locked herself inside and I told the deputy I had the keys. He took them from me, knocked on the window to get her attention, and started to unlock the door and open it. As he did, she came at him with an ink pen in her hand, trying to stab him. She failed and, in a moment, several other officers arrived and overtook her, putting her in handcuffs, placing her under arrest, then forcing her into the back of a squad car. She kept ranting and raving.

The deputies knew I was hurt, because I had told them I'd been hit, my hands were scraped, and I was smeared with dirt, but I was still standing and didn't have any obvious severe injuries.

"David, before you go to the hospital, do you mind filling out this report, while things are still fresh in your mind?" the deputy asked. I told him I would and leaned over to use the trunk of a second squad car as a desktop. I could barely manage writing, my hand was shaking so badly.

An officer walked over to the driver and asked her, "What are you doing here? Why'd you do this?"

"I'm here to do the stunt for the movie and, if it doesn't work, I'm supposed to kill myself," she said.

It was clear this was a mental health situation. After a few more moments, instead of taking her to jail, they took her off to a mental health facility.

As it turned out, one of her relatives worked in the Brewer's front office and knew a bit about her background. She had been battling mental illness for a long time and hadn't worked in something like twenty years. Over time, she had wandered away from her family. They had tried to help her but, since she was an adult, there was little they could force her to do. As I would learn later at a court hearing, apparently, when she was on medication, she was relatively stable but, when she wasn't, she was delusional. In recent years, she had become increasingly out of control. In 1991, she had been arrested for stalking the singer Julio Iglesias and, in 1993, had been arrested for threatening Queen Elizabeth, demanding to be adopted. The night before, she had actually been in Chicago, stalking Oprah and threatening to harm her. She had not been successful and had gotten away before doing any harm, but Oprah's security detail had gotten her license plate number and had a full description. It turns out she was still wearing the same clothes from the day before.

Had I known I had PTSD at the time, my first move, after getting myself checked out physically, would have been to see a therapist or a counselor, because I was a mess. Until that moment, shock and adrenaline had protected me from feeling the full brunt of the impact with the car but, as I completed the report, that began to wear away. I called Denise.

"You're not going to believe this, but I was just run over by a car on the baseball field. I hope I'm okay, but my right knee is very sore and I have a terrible headache." She said she would meet me at the hospital. I didn't want to go. I was in denial and afraid of what the doctors might find. If I didn't go, maybe I could pretend it never happened. Maybe it hadn't happened, and this was just another nightmare worse than the others.

Denise was adamant. She said, if I didn't agree to see the doctor, she would call an ambulance or come to the ballpark and take me to the hospital herself. I knew she was right, and I finally agreed to see the Brewers team doctor who, at that point, was also my knee surgeon. She said she'd bring the girls and meet me at his office. I asked Denise to call my mother to let her know what had happened. A friend from the grounds crew drove me to the doctor.

Then my mom called Denise. "Is David okay?" she asked.

Denise replied, "I think he's okay. I was about to call you." My mom explained that she was calling because a neighbor had just phoned her. She had been watching CNN and heard that a car had hit a groundskeeper at Milwaukee County Stadium. It couldn't have been more than twenty minutes after the accident.

As I waited in the doctor's office, my mind was scrambled. Flashbacks from the accident at McDonald's fifteen years before kept flooding into my thoughts, along with fresh new memories of what had just taken place. As the adrenaline wore off, my knee throbbed in intense pain, and my headache worsened. I just sat there, stunned. I felt completely disturbed and altered. Had this really happened? What would the doctor find? How bad was my knee? Would I need more surgeries? What in the world was the woman thinking? Who was she?

I said a brief prayer asking that my condition not be too serious. I'm not sure it helped. Time seemed to slow. I could hear the tick of each second on the wall clock, and each rapid beat of my heart. I felt as though I was in a bad dream and couldn't wake up.

It was another classic traumatic experience, the kind that we now know results in PTSD. Not only was the experience horrible on its own—getting hit by a car is a pretty big deal—but, just as had happened at McDonald's and at physical therapy, the initial experience took a long time to play itself out. I lay on the warning track, hurt and dazed, for at least several minutes, and I faced an oncoming car not once, but twice—the entire time, my levels of panic and fear peaking. I had no control over the situation and no explanation for it. And my support system, the emotional infrastructure that helped keep me going, wasn't available. Denise and the girls were home. It was made even worse by the fact that it was so similar to the incident at McDonald's. It almost felt otherworldly.

The nurse called me into the exam room and I snapped out of my deep trance. The doctor gave me a quick but thorough examination. Apart from some abrasions on my hands, kind of like road rash that must have been caused by landing on the warning track, I didn't look too bad on the outside but, inside, I was a mess.

After I told him what had happened, the doctor said he was surprised that I had made it. He said it was amazing what adrenaline can do and that, as much pain as I was beginning to experience now, that it would only get worse. He was mostly concerned with my right knee. He had performed surgery on me before and was familiar with it. He explained there was certainly damage, but until they did more tests, and the swelling went down, it would be impossible to know just how bad it was. How many times had I heard that?

He ordered the tests, put my knee in an immobilizer from my ankle to my thigh, gave me some crutches, and sent me home. Every moment was agonizing. Emotional and physical pain dominated my life, every second of every day.

Four days later, I appeared at a hearing at the mental hospital to testify. By law, the state could only keep the driver for seventy-two hours unless they held a hearing and determined she was a danger to herself or others. She wasn't there. Her attorney said she was in a straitjacket somewhere and had waived her right to appear.

Two days later, I attended a second hearing. This time, she was in court. Seeing her again did not help me. Being in her presence made me uneasy. I was just across the aisle, one row back, and, even though there was a deputy next to me, I didn't feel safe. I had to testify as to what happened, or else she might be released. The judge finally ruled that she would be held for six months, or until medication regulated her illness. The woman, who was already on her fifth attorney since the accident, reacted violently. She leapt up from her chair and started screaming profanities again. Her attorney said, "Sit down. That's not the way to act."

She put her finger in his face and said, "Don't tell me what to do. You fucking work for me."

I was too close. She turned and lunged toward me, gesturing wildly, violently waving her arm and pointing at me repeatedly with her finger. Then she yelled, "I want to know. How close did I come to hitting you? Did I miss you by one foot, two foot, or three foot? Because I always fucking miss at least ONE FOOT!"

The deputy sheriff reached for his mace, the judge slammed his gavel down and ordered the courtroom cleared. Security quickly pushed her to the floor and subdued her. I was overcome with fear. Right there, I had another intense flashback about being hit. To her, this was some crazy game, one only she understood. I realized she was ill, but it was hard to feel much compassion.

Incredibly, just as the driver at the McDonald's was never charged with a traffic violation and the physical therapist had not been held at fault and retained his position, a month later, the mentally ill woman, now responding to medication, was released from the facility. She was even allowed to keep her driver's license, as long as she could pass a driver's test while under medication. It did not seem possible.

I was shocked and bewildered. It caused me even more stress. How was it possible for her to get away with trespassing and hitting me with a car? Later, after considering legal action, I learned that she had terrorized another person with whom she had a run-in, showing up at the family home, marching back and forth in front of the house, and eventually trying to sue them herself, claiming she had been injured on their property. I was advised to leave her alone.

On the mound for Piqua, OH, Legion Post 184.

A memorable day pitching batting practice to Terry at Milwaukee County Stadium.

My dad, Bill Mellor, mowing the lawn in Newport, NH, 1947.

My grandfather, William H. "Big Bil Mellor. He played for the Baltimore in 1902.

My brothers Chip (left) and Terry (right), and me on my jumpy horse.

My love of the game started young. L did I know my glove was on the wron

On the mound for Piqua, OH, Legion Post 184.

A memorable day pitching batting practice to Terry at Milwaukee County Stadium.

My dad, Bill Mellor, mowing the lawn in Newport, NH, 1947.

My grandfather, William H. "Big Bill" Mellor. He played for the Baltimore Orioles in 1902.

My brothers Chip (left) and Terry (right), and me on my jumpy horse.

My love of the game started young. Little did I know my glove was on the wrong hand.

Courtesy of Troy Daily News

After the accident at McDonald's, from the Troy Daily News.

Alex helping me pass the time while recovering from one of my many knee surgeries.

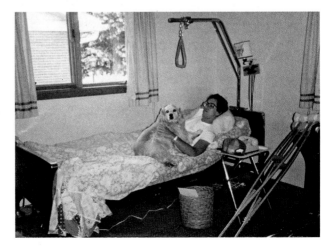

Joined with my best friend and wife, Denise, on our wedding day. November 1988.

The Mellor family at my wedding: Chip, me, my mother, Marj, and Terry.

Ron Vesley Photo

Talking turf with my daughters pregame. Milwaukee County Stadium.

Ron Vesley Photo

My daughters in their grounds crew uniforms helping pregame. Milwaukee County Stadium.

Grass pattern created for Flag Day.

Celebrating 2013 World Series win.

Sharing a laugh with Joe Mooney and some young Sox fans.

Courtesy of *Boston Herald*/Ted Fitzgerald

Marissa McClain/Boston Red Sox

2013 ALDS Opening Ceremony. B Strong grass pattern in the outfield with first respond-ers, marathon volunteers, and others impacted by the marathon bombing.

Celebrating the 2018 World Series win on a duck boat in the parade.

Courtesy of Pete Nesbit

Celebrating the 2018 World Series win on the field with Drago.

Billie Weiss Photo

Courtesy of Bryan Kroten

Watering the infield skin pregame at Fenway Park.

Showing the umpire updated radar loops between innings.

Billie Weiss Photo

Puppies at the Park. Family portrait of Lisle, Drago, and their 2018 litter on home plate. Keeper is in the blue bandanna.

Chapter 9

I was thirty-two years old. When I looked ahead, I found it difficult to imagine what kind of life lay before me. After being
struck again, every part of my body ached. My knee hurt worse than
ever and it was increasingly difficult to hide my psychological pain.
The volume on my flashbacks and nightmares had been turned all
the way up. Somehow—by blaming the chronic pain—I managed
to keep my symptoms hidden from those around me, but I needed
more surgery on my knee. Without it, I couldn't walk well enough
to do my job, and I couldn't fake my way through that. There was no
way to avoid it.

By now, every time I underwent surgery, the fact that I had
already been operated on so many times before was almost as problematic as the new issue. There was a ton of scar tissue and my knee
joint was slowly deteriorating, making it ever more difficult to reattach and rebuild the knee using my hamstring. If my knee was a
leaky boat, it was becoming all patches, with less and less of the
original structure remaining strong enough to support the repairs.
This time, I had damage to my ligaments and the joint. After an
injury, the body tries to heal itself by flooding the area with white

blood cells to combat the possibility of infection. In my case, the repetition of trauma resulted in the inflammation response being unable to turn itself off. At that point, healing can actually be inhibited, muscle growth slows, and pain is constant and pronounced.

The surgeon operated on my knee twice, each time trying to repair and reinforce my previous surgeries and make it possible for me to return to work. Neither surgery worked as well as we had hoped. Rehabilitation was long and laborious and, although I was able to return to work, the pain was excruciating. Pain medication couldn't even penetrate. Nothing worked to dull the pain.

I was difficult to live with before. Now I was worse. Not only was I in agony but, after each surgery, I rushed back to work as quickly as possible and stayed there as much as I could. It distracted me. Staying busy was the only way to keep from focusing on the pain. When I went home and had down time with Denise and the girls, it was completely different. Most people look forward to being off work, staying home and relaxing. I wanted to but, unfortunately, there were times there was nothing relaxing about it. Without work to focus on, I dwelled on the negative. As a result, when I was stressed, I would stay away as much as I could, which only made me feel guiltier and more ashamed of the fact that I felt like I was completely screwed up, a bad husband and father.

After the second surgery, it became clear I was not much better off that I had been before. I was still in intense pain. My doctor started talking to me about knee replacement. The surgery, which was developed in the late 1960s, had once seemed like science fiction, but was becoming more common. Still, at the time, it was considered "old person" surgery, usually performed on people in their sixties. That's because replacement knees only last so long. Some bone must be removed during surgery, making it possible to perform a total of only two replacements on one knee. Surgeons tried to get patients to wait as long as possible because, if a second replacement failed, the only remaining option at the time was to fuse the knee into one position, which can severely limit mobility. My doctor was blunt. He agreed that my knee joint needed to be replaced, but thought I was too young to have the surgery.

By the fall of 1996, a year after being hit a second time, I was only in my mid-thirties. I was in such agony that I went to see a knee replacement specialist anyway. He examined me and evaluated my condition. He agreed to the operation, though he, too, thought I was too young. It wasn't just a matter of age, but of lifestyle. Older people tend to be less active, so the replacement lasts longer. He told me that each replacement can only handle about ten thousand to fifteen thousand bends and, with my lifestyle, which entailed a great deal of physical work around the ballpark, I would likely use those up quickly, so, by the age of fifty or so, I could be looking at a total fusion. He recommended waiting as long as possible before having the surgery. He said I'd know from my pain, but my quality of life sucked. As far as I was concerned, it was almost non-existent. I could barely go up and down a set of stairs. It hurt to drive, to press the accelerator and to move my foot back and forth from the brake. It hurt to sit down in a chair and it hurt to get up. Physical pain was dominating my life as much as the emotional pain. At work, while I was busy, I could push it away but, away from the stadium, the last thing I wanted to do was something physical. The girls would want me to come outside and play or go somewhere with them and I wanted to, but I just couldn't do it as well or as often as I wanted to or as they needed. And then I'd start blaming myself, and either pull back or lash out in anger. It was a vicious cycle.

I told the doctor the pain was dominating the quality of my life and impacting my family's quality of life. I wanted the replacement now. I was missing the kids' lives and, if I didn't do something soon,

I might never be able to make it up. I thought, "I'm fifty and have a fused knee, fine. I'd rather have the surgery and gain some quality of life, be a better father now while the kids are young. I'd rather take that risk than continue to suffer, to just go to work, come home and not do anything with anyone." It was that simple.

Some of that was the PTSD talking. Not that I wasn't truly in pain, but I was using the pain as a shield, tricking myself into thinking that my problems—at least most of them—were due to knee pain, and not my other issues. I often wonder how many people are in the same position I was then, convincing themselves that their problems stem from one thing, rather than from untreated PTSD. If my story helps one person from going through the agony that I have, then I'll consider what I went through worth it. I would not wish what I was going through on my worst enemy in the world.

The surgeon agreed to do the surgery and scheduled it for the week after the Super Bowl. In 1995, the Packers' thirty-five-year lease to play at County Stadium had expired, and the team played all its home games in Green Bay. 1996 was the first year we didn't have to maintain the field in the fall and winter for football. The Packers had a great season and ended up meeting the Patriots in the Super Bowl. My brother Terry knew how miserable I was, because he flew an old friend of mine in for the weekend to watch the game with me and help distract me before the surgery. We had a blast watching the game together. That's another funny thing about PTSD. I tricked myself into thinking that no one close to me knew how badly off I was. But I hadn't—not really. Denise didn't know I had PTSD, but she knew something was going on, and so did Terry. The people around us are sometimes much more perceptive and understanding than we give them credit for. Most often, they are even more perceptive than we are. After the Packers beat the Patriots 35-21, my buddies on the grounds crew joked that it was too bad they no longer played at Country Stadium. If they had, maybe we would have gotten Super Bowl rings.

The next week, I had knee replacement surgery. It was anything but routine. In a normal surgery, the incision is straight up the middle of the knee, right over the kneecap. But my right knee had already been opened up on both sides—I had foot-long scars to prove it, and those scars disrupted the normal flow of blood in and around the joint. If the surgeon went right up the middle, they were afraid there wouldn't be enough blood flow remaining and that the skin could die. If that happened, I might be looking at amputation. The only alternative was to go in from the side, to extend and reopen the earlier incision, making it longer and curved, creating a large flap. To work on the joint, he just flipped open the flap. Because the bone had deteriorated, the joint no longer operated smoothly. From there, he removed damaged portions of the end of both the tibia and the fibula and affixed metal and plastic replacements to the end of the bone before replacing the back of my real kneecap with an artificial one. After that, ligaments and tendon transplants were reattached as needed, the doctor manipulated the new knee to make certain it operated smoothly, and then the incision was closed. In about 90 percent of patients, pain relief is immediate and often dramatic.

I was not a member of the ninety percent club. There was so much scar tissue due to my seventeen previous surgeries that, even after the replacement, my knee just wouldn't bend the way it was supposed to. Everything was just too tight.

When I woke from the anesthesia, I could not believe the pain I was in. I thought I had known pain before, but this was an entirely new beast. And this was while I was still on an IV. I was absolutely miserable. I'd been told the surgery might be tougher for me than someone whose knee was not as damaged as mine, but this was beyond my imagination.

Looking back, I wish I would have stayed in the hospital longer and had access to pain medication, but the thinking then was to get me out of the hospital as quickly as possible to start the rehabilitation process. After knee replacements, doctors want you moving your knee during healing to retain the knee's range of motion. When they sent me home, they also gave me a passive machine. While resting, my knee was supposed to be in the machine, so it was moving and did not allow scar tissue to form. Despite the pain, I prepared to go home. But, first, I had to learn to administer a blood thinner to myself, something commonly prescribed to knee replacement patients to keep blood clots from forming. Unfortunately, I have an almost pathological fear of needles. As a nurse tried to teach me how to give myself a shot in the stomach, it took me nearly ten long minutes to finally break through my skin with the needle. I was sweating bullets the whole time. When it finally went in, I realized it wasn't such a big deal after all and laughed out loud. Maybe this recovery wouldn't be too bad.

I went home, armed with pain medication and the passive motion machine. Over the next three days, I was in varying degrees of misery. It hurt to remain still but, after I strapped my knee into the machine and it started to make everything bend, I wanted to tear my head off. Recovery was supposed to be quick. There was supposed to be some discomfort, but it wasn't supposed to last very long. In my case, it seemed to be going in the opposite direction. My pain wasn't going down and my range of motion was not increasing. By the third day, my knee had swollen to the size of a basketball. I couldn't take it anymore. Denise took me to see the doctor. He thought the knee had filled with fluid and that perhaps the scar tissue was keeping it from draining properly. He decided to drain it with a large needle, something they normally wouldn't do due for fear of infection. The last thing you want is to put something foreign into the joint, but my knee was so swollen he had to act. It looked like the skin was ready to pop.

I was lying down on the examination table when he stuck the large needle into my knee. On his first attempt, he hit the edge of my kneecap. My body spasmed from the pain like I was some kind of cartoon character, leaving only my heels and head touching the table as my back arched awkwardly. This caused the needle to strike the same spot a second time, only harder. It hurt so badly I could hardly breathe. I settled down and he tried again. This time the needle went in, but instead of filling with blood and fluid and bringing me some relief, very little came out. He concluded that despite the blood thinners, the joint had filled with blood and it had coagulated, perhaps due to my poor circulation. There was little he could do. My body would just have to reabsorb the fluid, which would take months, cause some pain, and suppress the joint's range of motion. Had I known of all the pain and suffering the surgery would cause, I'm not certain I would have gone through with it, but I would have done anything to be a better husband and father.

Six days after surgery, I had a post-op meeting with my doctor. Despite spending agonizing hours on the range of motion machine, I was losing mobility. As the surgeon examined my knee, he concluded that the scar tissue was so strong it was preventing my knee from bending. He decided to put me under anesthetic for a "physical manipulation" of my knee. That's a nice way of saying he would put me under before physically forcing my leg to bend, using all the strength he could muster, hoping to tear the scar tissue loose. The procedure is so violent, the doctor monitors it on a fluoroscope (a live x-ray) to make sure he doesn't inadvertently break either the thighbone or one of the shinbones. That's how much force is required.

When I awoke after the procedure, my knee did move a bit more than before but, incredibly, I was in even more pain. The powerful pain medication they gave me had no impact. It was so bad I could sleep in only ten or fifteen-minute intervals. Over the course of a day, I would maybe get two hours of sleep.

Needless to say, my PTSD symptoms were on overdrive. The accident left me incredibly anxious. Coupled with the pain and exhaustion, every waking moment was agony. I hadn't slept well before. Now, between the drugs and the pain, not only was I not sleeping but, while trying to sleep, I was experiencing intense flashbacks, not just of McDonald's and PT, but also of the event at County Stadium. It was like my brain was looking for a place to put it. The nightmares were more frequent, more intense, and more debilitating. Asleep or awake, I was in anguish. It was hard for me to imagine living this way for the rest of my life.

I wonder now why no one ever said anything, why counseling of some kind was never suggested, not because anyone thought I had PTSD, but simply because of all the stress I was going through. In part, I think it was because everything wrong with me was still viewed through the lens of medicine, as physical issues. I had so many that I think it was hard for anyone to see past them. And I didn't allow them to see past them. I had become so adept at deflecting any concerns, at blaming everything on the physical pain, I think everyone around me followed my lead.

I never tried to harm or kill myself. But, after the manipulation, there was one night I was so miserable that I wished I would die before suffering another minute. I hoped I would not wake up and, that night, I prayed and tried to make a pact with God. If I was allowed to die, all I asked was that Denise and the girls could move forward without the hardships I knew that my own mother experienced after my father died, or the emotional loss my brothers and I felt going through our lives without a father. At that moment, I truly believed they would be better off without me. These were my final thoughts as I drifted into a fitful sleep early that morning, hoping I would never wake again, and never again feel this kind of pain.

Later that morning, my eyes fluttered open. I was alive, but deeply ashamed about hoping that I would die. I prayed to God and thanked him. No matter what I was going through, I realized that worrying about my own pain and putting that above the needs of my family was selfish. My misplaced pride and stubbornness had clouded my thinking and prevented me from admitting that I was incredibly depressed and unable to keep things in perspective.

I was mixed up inside. I was fighting flashbacks, recurring nightmares, insomnia, and exhaustion so profound it was affecting my memory. I argued with myself relentlessly, angry that I wasn't in control, and beat myself up over things I couldn't do anything about. I suffered night sweats, trembled with anxiety, clenched my jaw so tight from the pain that my face often felt as if it had been punched, and my head felt like I'd been banging it against walls for years. Loud noises triggered almost instantaneous headaches. And I worried constantly, always afraid that something was about to go wrong for my family or me. It was overwhelming.

I didn't know what to do. I didn't know how to explain my physical or emotional pain. I was scared of the person I was becoming. I barely spoke to Denise, the kids, or anyone. I was embarrassed and felt like a burden. I needed help with the simplest things. The fact that I knew I wasn't a good husband or father tore me up. The self-recrimination was endless. Any positive thought I had was rapidly swept away by a thousand negative ones. I had become a profoundly unhappy person, spreading my sadness over everyone. Even worse, despite all the internal monologues, I couldn't summon any words at all to articulate my feelings. I was afraid to let anybody get a glimpse of the prison I was in. I didn't trust anyone with the knowledge of what was happening to me. I was surrounded by love and support, yet I felt totally alone. No one knew what was happening in my head and in my heart. When I was around others, I really wasn't present, I was just acting.

Everyone knew I wasn't feeling well but, since I wasn't being honest, they were only assuming what was wrong—the knee, the pain, the exhaustion. It was all of that and so much more. I was still ignorant to the root cause. I worried that, if anyone found out how messed up I was inside, I'd be viewed as crazy or soft. Fortunately, I had reached a breaking point. I broke down and told Denise how awful I felt, that she and the girls would be better off without me. I didn't tell her about my emotional pain but, for the first time ever, I cut loose and told her about just how much physical pain I was in, how bad I felt, and how desperate I was becoming. I cried and cried and cried, years of frustration pouring out of me.

It scared Denise and, although I didn't realize it then, that was the proper response. She rightfully concluded that I was clinically depressed and needed help. We saw a doctor the next day. She told him what I had said and detailed my behavior. I was furious. I thought she had broken our trust. I shut down completely, promising myself I would never again allow my feelings to come to the surface. The shame I felt was overwhelming.

The doctor insisted that I see a psychiatrist. We made an appointment. I went once. I was so scared and embarrassed that I never went back. I refused to give it a chance. To think now of the years of suffering that might have been avoided if I'd accepted the challenge is frustrating and heartbreaking.

Yet again, I opted to go it alone. I tried to find reasons to continue and thought of those I loved and those who inspired me, like the double amputee I'd watched that day in physical therapy so many years before. I decided the only way to function was to carry on in spite of it all, and simply live with the demons and burdens

I had amassed since being hit at McDonald's. I continued to pray that, someday, I would open up and find help, which would not only help me but, most importantly, help my family, who I loved more than words can describe. I was determined to turn things around. I buried my feelings even deeper. Ever so slowly, I started to pull the rest of me back out.

Four days after the initial manipulation, my knee was nearly frozen in place. I needed another one. The doctor was worried not only about the pain, but whether my bones were strong enough to handle it. He'd have to apply even more force this time. Unfortunately, he didn't see any other alternative. Without another manipulation, my leg would likely be stiff for the remainder of my life. How could I ever be the husband and father I wanted to be? How could I ever be a groundskeeper if I couldn't bend down and touch the ground? I feared becoming an even greater burden on everyone.

My mind flooded with fears, not just about the procedure, but about the remainder of my life. I felt paralyzed by anxiety. It was like being afraid of heights and standing on the edge of a diving board, unable to go back and unable to go forward. I finally said yes. There was no other option.

As unbelievable as it may seem, I awoke from the procedure to an entirely new level of pain. Whatever medication I was on may as well have been water and sugar. It had no effective impact.

The surgeon said the scar issue was stronger than before and that, at one point, he worried that he had broken my thighbone. I almost wished he had. That couldn't be any worse than what I was experiencing.

The manipulation was successful, and the scar tissues broke free but the recovery was long and drawn out. For the first few weeks, between the pain, drugs, lack of sleep, nightmares, and panic attacks, life was unbearable. Any sense of normalcy seemed completely out of reach, impossible. I was almost living in another dimension.

Fortunately, as my body reabsorbed the coagulated blood, I began to make slow, physical progress. If I could walk and work again, it would be easier to pretend everything was back to normal. Over the next several months, I underwent physical therapy up to five days a week to build strength and range of motion. I saw other knee replacement patients make quick recoveries and was embarrassed at my own slow pace. Once again, I had to learn to walk "normal" again. My body didn't want to listen to my brain and, after being on crutches for so long, wanted to land toe-first. Like some of the other knee replacement patients, I first learned to walk on a treadmill in water to put less stress on my knee joint. I then progressed to walking slowly on a treadmill in front of a mirror, so I could see the movement of my foot and leg. When I started to see improvements in my walking stride, I took this as a sign of great things to come. While I was amazed at how difficult it was for my leg to start walking "normal" again, I was excited to see and experience even the smallest improvements. Each positive step forward was empowering.

As had happened before, my competitive side returned and I, once again, managed to focus on my "one-base-at-a-time" philosophy. It wasn't as simple as flipping a light switch, but I went back to the strategies that had helped me before. Although I realize now I still wasn't addressing the underlying cause of so much of my trouble, at least it allowed me to put even the smallest improvements into better perspective. I started to think of not only short-term goals but long-term goals too.

My recovery was aided immensely by the work of my masseuse. I underwent a regimen of deep tissue massage to break up scar tissue and keep my muscles supple. That was its own kind of agony, but the results were profound. I consider her a gift from God. I would never have made it without her.

The months it took to finally get back to walking were some of the most physically and emotionally challenging periods in my life. I did all I could to turn my pain into a learning tool. During my time at hospitals and in physical therapy departments, every time I saw other people dealing with even more serious and painful challenges, I reminded myself how fortunate I was. I learned a lot about personal growth and what the human body, mind, and soul can overcome. There were many sleepless days and nights when I had deep bone pain so powerful that I could not even focus my eyes to watch TV, yet I forced myself, at least outwardly, to stay positive.

This surgery and recovery had thrown me for a loop. My faith was challenged more than ever. I decided it was up to me to reach down deep into my inner spirit and summon the strength to not give up. I felt I owed it to my wonderful wife and two amazing daughters to make the best of the situation. After all the sacrifices they had made for me, I had to find the strength to do the same for them.

After months of rehabilitation, I was finally able to go back to work on a limited basis. I finally started to feel "normal" again, or at least what passed for normal. It was wonderful to be back in the flow of life.

My knee was functional but looked horrible. Now I had even more multi-colored scarring to go along with sunken areas due to atrophy and missing tendons. I became self-conscious when I noticed people staring but, now, instead of getting angry or feeling ashamed, I employed a new strategy. I told stories.

The first story went something like this: "I was golfing a great round on TPC Sawgrass in Florida, when I hit a long drive into deep rough near a water hazard. As I was preparing for the next shot, an eight-foot alligator clamped down on my right knee. I fought him off with my nine iron and, eventually, had boots made out of his hide." That got some raised eyebrows. Then I'd tell a second story. "Okay, here's what really happened. I was enjoying a beautiful day snorkeling when a great white rubbed up against me. I tried to swim away but he came around and bit down on my knee. I flailed at it with my swim mask but couldn't shake free. Then, angry and frightened, I used all my strength to punch the hungry beast in the nose. The shark let go and swam off as my friends arrived to rescue me. I haven't been able to watch *Jaws* since." If they were still skeptical, I'd tell them the truth.

Funny enough, people's responses were often, "So, what hole were you on?" or, "How big was the shark?" The truth is stranger than fiction.

Chapter 10

On Saturday, March 22, we met with the grounds crew to welcome them to the start of the new season, go over rules, and answer any of their questions. I enjoyed talking shop and being back with everyone. Afterwards, I went into my office to elevate my knee at my desk for a few minutes before driving home. Shortly thereafter, several veteran members from the crew came into my office. They appeared concerned and asked if I was ok. I said I felt fine and asked what was on their minds. They explained that, at various times during the meeting, I stuttered, seemed confused, and didn't make sense. I hadn't noticed any of that. I told them I felt fine, thanked them for their concern, and drove home. I was puzzled. I felt totally normal.

At home, I sat on the couch with Denise and Cacky and put my foot up on an old trunk we used as a coffee table. We started talking about the day each of us had had, and the next thing I remember is Denise leaning over me trying to get me to snap out of it. I didn't know what was happening. She told me I had just had some kind of seizure, that my legs spasmed so violently that I had kicked the coffee table across the room. An ambulance was on the way.

I was rushed to the emergency room, but the episode had passed. Doctors ran a battery of tests on me but discovered nothing. Over the next few months, I continued to have periodic seizures and saw a series of specialists, but no one could determine the cause. I hadn't had a stroke, I didn't have epilepsy, and I didn't have a brain tumor. As a precaution, I stopped driving. Denise and my boss took turns ferrying me back and forth to work.

The fear of having a seizure added to my anxiety and increased the isolation I felt from others. In my mind, this was just more evidence of how screwed up I was. The only comfort, really, came from our dog, Buddy, a Brittany spaniel.

Denise discovered that Buddy could sense when a seizure was coming. He would lay down on top of me, as if weighing me down and trying to prevent me from moving and hurting myself. He would remain on top of me until the seizure passed. It was a great relief to know in advance that a seizure was about to happen. He never had a false alarm, and never laid on me like that unless a seizure was imminent.

Buddy was fantastic, but I couldn't take him everywhere I went, and I didn't always experience warning symptoms before a seizure started. Sometimes I giggled for no reason before I had a seizure or experienced brief tremors, but not always. Denise eventually noticed that the seizures seemed to come after stressful events. I would be fine during the situation but, afterward, as I started to relax, I often slipped into a seizure.

This gave me one more behavior I wanted to keep hidden from everyone, one more anxiety to keep at bay. One time, my aunt and mother were in a car accident in South Carolina. Terry and I chartered a plane to get there as a quickly as possible. It was a grueling trip. The pilot landed at the wrong airport and left us stranded in the middle of the night in some out-of-the-way town in *North*

Carolina. It was impossible to rent a car, so we ended up taking a cab for hundreds of miles to get to the hospital.

When we arrived, we were relieved to learn that my aunt and mother were not nearly as badly hurt as we initially feared. The nurses at the hospital let me lay down on a bed to rest and, a few moments later, I went into a seizure. When I came to my senses, I looked around to make sure no one had seen what had happened. They hadn't. I felt there was enough stuff going on already and the last thing I wanted to do was draw attention to myself, so I didn't tell anyone. I was on edge the rest of the trip, afraid of what would happen if I had a seizure in front of my mom, my aunt, or Terry. I didn't but continued to suffer periodic seizures into the fall.

If not for Denise, I might still be having them. One day at the doctor's office, she was leafing through a medical journal and noticed a story that mentioned the pain medication my doctor had prescribed. The article noted that, in some patients, it caused seizures, both by itself and in combination with some other drugs, such as muscle relaxers. Sure enough, I was also taking a muscle relaxer, as I was prone to cramping up. Denise brought it to attention of my doctor. He reviewed the literature and came to the same conclusion she had. My doctor changed my medication and I have not had a seizure since. It would not be the last time that browsing through a magazine in a waiting room would have a dramatic impact on my life.

Denise is one of the brightest and most perceptive people I've ever known. If she ever decided to go back to college and get a degree, I have no doubt that she could become a doctor, lawyer, nuclear physicist, or anything else. She's that intelligent. Instead, she's dedicated herself to taking care of me and the girls. In my case, that's been challenging enough.

The Brewers, from team owner Bud Selig to my boss Gary, could not have been more sympathetic to my situation. Not once did they try to rush me back to work too soon or move to replace me while I was missing time. No one ever complained that I was getting any kind of special treatment. The Brewer's treated all their employees fairly and compassionately.

My reputation in the groundskeeping community did not suffer from my repeated absences either. Everyone seemed to understand that none of these issues were my own doing, that I always did everything I could to get back on the field as quickly as possible, and that I never made excuses or shied away from my share of the work. I always took my job seriously, and others recognized that. I continued to be offered other head groundskeeping jobs in baseball. Some were very tempting.

When George Toma, the legendary groundskeeper of the Kansas City Royals, decided to step down, he called and told me I had first refusal. The Royals had decided to remove their artificial turf and install a grass field. It was a terrific opportunity, and I flew out for an interview. They wanted me to start right away, but I had some work and responsibilities to wrap up in Milwaukee and had committed to finishing the football season. I asked if they would fly me out for the weekends for a short while, so I could finish my work in Milwaukee while beginning my responsibilities in Kansas City. They were fine with that, but when I asked if Denise could come with me and if they could recommend a realtor so she could start house hunting, the club executive I was dealing with reacted as if I had asked him for the moon. In fact, he got angry with me, and told me they would "allow" her to stay in my hotel room, but that I would have to pay for all her travel expenses and that finding a realtor was not their responsibility. This was nothing like the family atmosphere the

Brewers fostered. After discussing it with Denise and my brothers, I turned the Royals down.

Anytime I faced an important decision, I consulted my family, no one more so than my brother Terry. Though both Chip and Terry stepped up after our father died, Terry, in part because he was around, bore the brunt of the responsibility of raising me. He taught me how to be a man and how to treat people with compassion and respect, no matter who they are.

At one point, Terry accepted the job of president of a bank in Chicago. The day before he was to start working, he mowed his lawn, did a bunch of yardwork, and decided to go visit the local branch in the grubby T-shirt and gym shorts in which he'd been working, just to see how he was treated. From the moment he walked into the bank, he could tell the employees were looking down on him because he wasn't dressed up like most of the other customers in the bank. When he explained that he wanted to open a checking account with the minimum amount, he was treated rudely. When he walked in the next day in a fine suit, they were shocked. He told them "You never know who you're talking to. It shouldn't matter how they're dressed. You don't want to judge a book by its cover. Treat everybody with respect, the way you want to be treated."

That's who Terry was. He taught me how to turn situations like that into opportunities to teach. He didn't go in the next day screaming and yelling, looking to humiliate anybody. He said, "This is an opportunity for us to learn and be a stronger team together." I think of that often. Growing up, my mom often spoke about how well my father treated people when he was vice president of the woolen mill, how he tried to have a connection with people throughout the plant, not just because he was the manager, but because he was a human being. Terry was able to pass my Dad's lesson down to me. He just believed in helping people. He was selfless. He brought my buddy in for the Super Bowl and, after my knee replacement, he sent us all to Disney World. The youngest person in Wisconsin to ever be hired as a bank president, he was a beloved boss and mentor to many and was named Wisconsin Special Olympics volunteer of the year in 1998. He taught me to give my best and take pride in attention to detail in all I do. It was from Terry that I learned how to mow a lawn and to add curb appeal through hard work. His energy and love of life was infectious. Terry guided me through my life, always leading by example.

In July of 1998, we spent a weekend together on the lake where they lived. It was beautiful. Terry, who was like another dad to the girls, took them bass fishing. On Sunday afternoon, we said our usual goodbyes, "I'll see you later," that kind of thing. We loved each other but were not especially verbal about our feelings.

Two days later, Pat, my sister-in-law, called.

"Terry is gone," she said.

"Where did he go?" I asked.

That's not what she meant. She explained that she arrived home to find Terry's dog going nuts, bouncing off the windows and trying desperately to get outside. She looked out and saw Terry lying on the grass, dead from a heart attack. As she spoke those words, I almost passed out. I went into shock. I felt my world crashing down and was consumed by grief.

I had no idea how to deal with his loss. I was so emotionally fragile that this became a trauma as debilitating as my previous traumatic incidents, more powerful and complicated than any pain I had ever experienced. All the barricades I had built up to protect myself collapsed. Before, I had a relatively small and specific set of triggers. Now, anything that reminded me of Terry caused a flashback or panic attack. So much of who I was had been wrapped in what Terry had taught me. Just navigating a normal day would involve negotiating a gauntlet of triggers. Everyday sights and sounds could send me reeling. If I drove past some place I'd been to with Terry I would explode in tears, crying so long and hard that eventually no more tears could come out. I felt like I was always on the edge of tears, a volcano of deep and complex emotions that seemed about to career out of control. Then I'd suck it up and either go back to work or go home and try to pretend everything was fine, that I was okay. I wasn't. I felt so incredibly guilty because I had never really told Terry how much he meant to me, how much I appreciated him, and how much I loved him.

That's PTSD for you. Today, of course, even though I never expressed my feelings toward Terry in words, I believe he knew how I felt. PTSD caused me to suppress my feelings, to turn my guilt inward, and make an already painful emotional experience far worse. One of the reasons I have decided to tell my story is that I want everyone who reads this book to call their loved ones today, as soon as you finish this paragraph to say, "Thank you" and, "I love you." Let them know how you feel about them and how important they are in your life.

I wish I had done that before Terry died. Life happens so quickly and I missed my opportunities, caught up in the rush of my day-to-day responsibilities. I should have known better, having lost my dad at such a young age. Instead, I learned my lesson the hard way, by undergoing years of self-recrimination and guilt. I hope you never have to deal with the same guilty feelings because they do significant damage to your psyche. I wish I had dealt with all my emotions sooner, because I let them fester inside me and grow to a point where they were bigger, stronger, and much worse in my mind than they really were. I let these emotions control me for too long, hurting everyone closest to me.

Fortunately, I have many wonderful memories of Terry and our time together—not just when we were younger, but as adults. Once, I brought him to Country Stadium and threw batting practice to him. Despite the condition of my knee, I could still throw strikes. Terry was always a pretty good hitter and we really went at it. I didn't lob too many cookies over the middle of the plate, that's for sure. I didn't make it to the majors as a player, but at least Terry got to see me pitch off the mound once.

He continues to inspire me. I try to honor his memory by moving forward and celebrating my life each day. He would give the shirt off his back to help somebody before he'd help himself, so I've established some scholarships in his name. One, through the National Sports Turf Managers Association, pays for a student to attend the national conference and continue their education. The second, here in New England, is for a member of a grounds crew. It could be someone working for a small town, a high school or a college, who has been recommended by their supervisor, who has a strong work ethic and would like to continue their education.

I still miss him dearly. He's a big part of why I kept turning down jobs. Staying in Milwaukee kept Terry close, even after he passed away. He was that important to me.

Although I might have been a mess at times at home, or alone, I managed to keep it together at work. The scientific approach I brought to the field proved effective and the results were noticeable to everyone, particularly now that we had made field design a regular part of our work. Not that we always did something particularly special but, over time, we became more and more adept at making even the simplest designs and patterns look striking.

In November of 2000, the Cincinnati Reds contacted me. The Brewers' new park, Miller Park, was nearing completion and would open in 2001. Gary and I had played a role in the design of the field, and it had been an incredible experience to be in on the planning from the initial stages. The Reds had just decided to replace the AstroTurf at old Riverfront Stadium and install a grass field. They wanted me to take over the new field at Riverfront while they made plans for a new ballpark. They wanted me to be involved in the planning process. It was a tempting offer. Riverfront was the first major league park I ever visited. I had gone there with Chip and Terry and, even though it wasn't the prettiest place in the world, it held an awful lot of good memories for me. And Ohio was home. Although my Mom had since moved back to South Carolina to be close to her family, most of Denise's family was still there and I knew she and the girls would enjoy being close to them. The Reds were incredibly friendly during negotiations. I was flattered by their interest, but Denise and I discussed it and I politely turned them down. They wouldn't take "No" for an answer. They asked me to withhold making a final decision and negotiate for another week. They had been so nice to this point I had to say yes.

The following Wednesday, my phone rang. I recognized the voice on the other end immediately. It was legendary groundskeeper Joe Mooney, the man who had taken care of Fenway Park for the last three decades or so.

"Hey, David," he barked. "I'm thinking about retiring, but I'll only retire if you replace me. You want to come and replace me? Job's yours if you want it."

Chapter 11

y dream job had always been to work for the Boston Red Sox. Joe Mooney was a fixture there, as much a part of the ballpark as the Green Monster. I had no idea he was planning to leave. I was blown away.

I'd known Mr. Mooney for several years through the network of groundskeepers, and I'd always liked and respected him. I never forgot how kind he had been to respond to the letter I had sent many years before. We finally met in person in 1993 when the Patriots wanted to talk to me about becoming their groundskeeper. I couldn't go to Boston without stopping at Fenway and saying hello, so I dropped by and had maybe a five-minute conversation with him.

Later, in 1995, the Patriots brought me back out and I stopped by again. Joe came over and said "Hey, Dave. Good to see ya."

Just as we started talking, a guy from his crew walked up and said, "Joe, Joe, you gotta go."

He said, "Hey, I'm talking to David."

But the other guy said, "No, you have to go. Your wife just died." I felt so bad for him.

We remained in contact after that. He was a man of few words, so I wouldn't call very often, because I knew he was always doing something, and I didn't want to interrupt him. More often, I'd just drop a card in the mail or write a brief note. Sometimes even the smallest gestures mean a great deal.

When I got that call from him, my heart leapt into my throat and my heart started pounding. It was the ultimate job offer, the ultimate opportunity.

"Oh, my gosh, Mr. Mooney," I said. "I'm incredibly interested. I'm flattered and honored to have the opportunity to follow in your footsteps." Then I started to process what needed to take place before I could accept. "I need to have a final package offer from the club, so I can weigh this out. Not only do I have the job with the Brewers right now, which I love, but the Cincinnati Reds offered me a job, and I have to give them an answer on Saturday." Clearly, I couldn't work for three teams at the same time!

"All right," he said. "I'll have John Buckley, the club president, call you."

I called Denise straight away. She knew that we were moving to Boston, no matter what. She knew what it meant to me.

Two days later, the Red Sox flew me out to Boston. I said hello to Joe, then met with John Buckley. As soon as we were alone, Mr. Buckley said, "David, this isn't an interview. The job's yours if you want it. We know what you can do for us. But, more importantly, what can we do to help Denise and your kids make this move successful?" I was blown away again. Only the Brewers and Billy Beane of the A's had made family such a priority before. Any smidgen of concern over taking the job quickly disappeared.

After the meeting, another gentleman dropped by and gave me a tour of the ballpark. I had been to Fenway before, but this time was different. Then, I'd felt like a visitor. This was like coming home.

It was November, so much of the field was covered with felt, and I was allowed to walk around. Had it not been covered, I probably would not have been allowed to do that. Mr. Mooney was a stickler about not letting people walk on the field who had no practical reason to do so. I knew the place well, but this was like looking at it with fresh eyes. I remember peering up at the upper deck and seeing all the playoff and World Series banners, memories of some of those series still etched in my brain and in my heart. Then I took in the retired numbers in right field, 9, 4, 1, 8, 42 for Ted Williams, Bobby Doerr, Joe Cronin, Carl Yazstremski, and Jackie Robinson. There was the Pesky pole in right field, the red seat in the bleachers, the Citgo sign looming over the Green Monster, and the foul pole atop the wall in left where Carlton Fisk hit that famous home run in game six of the 1975 World Series. Here was where Babe Ruth pitched, where Ted Williams and Jim Rice patrolled left field, where Luis Tiant taught every kid in New England how to turn their backs to the hitter, and where Dwight Evans displayed one of the best arms in baseball. Here is where baseball history still lived. All my childhood memories of seeing Fenway on TV, of my brothers telling me about the time they went to a game with my Dad, playing Wiffle ball in the backyard while pretending I was here, imagining that I was on the mound throwing the last pitch to win the World Series, came flooding in. And now I was here, on the field of my dreams. It felt magical.

All of a sudden, I stumbled. I stepped in a hole that I couldn't see through the felt. *What was that?* I thought. I didn't want them to think I was disrespectful, but I couldn't imagine why there was a hole in left field, so I casually mentioned it. The guy said, "Oh, yeah, that's one of the drains." Joe was creative working with what he had to try to help with drainage problems. He added drains with removable quick caps in areas of the field where he had the biggest drainage challenges. That's when I realized I'd be going from the newest field in the majors, to one of the oldest. In Milwaukee, everything was state of the art. Fenway Park had been here since 1912. It would be a challenge, but one I'd often dreamed of.

I accepted Boston's offer the next day. We moved to Boston on Christmas Eve, into a house we'd rented in the suburbs. I was able to make arrangements to have a little Christmas tree waiting for us, and I stopped at a store on the way to pick up some stocking stuffers for the kids. It was a wonderful Christmas. I had everything I wanted, at least everything I knew to ask for.

I wasn't supposed to start for a few more weeks, but Mr. Mooney was on vacation, so I started that week. They gave me an office. I settled in and got to know the crew. I needed to work and stay busy. The Red Sox never asked me about my health issues, but they certainly knew that I had knee trouble. There were times I still wore the brace for extra support and, although I tried hard not to limp, I knew there were times I still did. But I was hired more for my brain, for my experience, than my brawn. And I sure as hell didn't bring up my other issues, the flashbacks and nightmares. That was too private to speak to anyone about.

Right after I accepted the job, my mom said, "You know, David, you're going to have to get used to how much ice is out there. You've dealt with a lot of snow in Ohio and Milwaukee but, in New England, especially Boston, there's a lot more ice, because of freezing fog and ice storms."

I was like, "Yeah, Mom. Thanks." I didn't really pay it much attention. Well, you know what they say: "Mom knows best." A week or two after I started, we got some storms and two or three inches of ice formed on the warning track and migrated into foul territory. Snow is a great insulator for grass, but ice suffocates it. It can really harm it, if not kill it completely.

It was Joe Mooney's first day back from vacation, and the first thing he noticed when he went out to the field was the ice. Joe has a colorful vocabulary, and he used most of it. His bark was way worse than his bite. If he liked you, he would do anything for you. He became a grandfather to my girls, and they just loved him. But he could be gruff, and the ice set him off. He got the crew out there to chop it up. No, let's put it this way. Joe went out there to chop the ice free and the rest of us tried to keep up with him. He seemed bionic. He chopped ice for eight hours straight, with a ten-minute break in the morning and a twenty-nine-minute break for lunch.

Our work day in the offseason was from 7:00 a.m. to 3:00 p.m. I remember coming home so exhausted that I could barely move after trying to keep up with Joe. At seventy-two years old, he was a wearing out all the eighteen-year-olds on the crew. He was a machine! I thought to myself, "This guy is incredible!" He stayed at the park during the transition, teaching me about all the quirks to a field that hadn't seen a major renovation since 1934. But Joe wasn't all work and no play.

That first day, he told me one challenge at Fenway was that, "When it really rains hard the dugouts will flood." I had seen that in Milwaukee at County Stadium, so I just nodded and continued listening. He then said, "When it really, really rains hard, the city storm drainage system backs up and the rain water comes up through the manhole covers in the Fenway concourse." I said that was interesting since I hadn't heard of that happening at a stadium before. He then said, "If it really, really, really rains hard, the first base camera well fills up with flood water and fish from the Charles River (approximately two miles away) swim through the drain pipes, into the camera pit, and then out onto the field." I didn't believe him, but out of respect, I just nodded my head.

Later that day, I went home and I told my wife, "You wouldn't believe the wild stories that Mr. Mooney tells."

Fast forward to the Friday night before opening day in April. The overnight forecast was for thunderstorms with the potential of between up to two to three inches of rain by morning. We put the tarp on to protect the infield skin and, by the time it stopped raining the next morning, nearly three inches had fallen. I walked out from my office under the stands behind third base, through the stands, and onto the warning track by the visitors' dugout, then around behind home plate. As I neared the home dugout, I looked down...and saw a fish lying on the grass! I couldn't believe my eyes! I thought Joe was pulling a prank on me or I was on Candid Camera or something. I looked around for Joe hiding somewhere in the park, but he was nowhere to be found. I walked over toward the first base camera pit and, sure enough, it was full of water all the way to the top. I looked out at the field and saw seven more fish laying on the tarp between the camera pit and where the second baseman plays. I took a photo of a fish, but now I wish I had saved a few and had them dry mounted, one for our owner, one for Joe, and one for my office, and one for home. How's that for a fish story? I never doubted Mr. Mooney again.

It could have been awkward for him to turn over control to another person, but he never made me feel the least bit uncomfortable or out of place. I hope that, one day, I can be as gracious as he was. On that very first day, he said "David, it's your field. We hired you. I want you here because I know you're the man. You can take over. If I can help you, let me know." He was amazing, an open book to me, without a hint of jealousy or ego. When I needed to ask him anything, he was there with an answer, and happy to give his opinion, but he never tried to interfere. I can't imagine being in that position and handling things better than the way he did with me.

More than that, though, he became family. He helped me and Denise and the girls in every way possible. I'd bring them all to the park and, the next thing I'd know, Mr. Mooney would be taking the girls to McDonald's or out for ice cream, holding their hands while they crossed the street. He stayed on for several years, not on the grounds crew, but in the maintenance department, and was always available to me whenever I needed him. That's what he wanted to do; stay around the ballpark. That's how much he loved it.

Chapter 12

At an old field like Fenway, there is always plenty to do. There hadn't been a major renovation since 1934. There was no automatic irrigation system, and the field had a pronounced crown to allow for drainage. The middle of the infield was eighteen inches higher than it was in foul territory. If you were in the dugout and looked out toward the outfield, you could only see the outfielder from the waist up. The grass was about 70 percent annual bluegrass, a shallow-rooted, lime-green grass that is prone to disease. It's not a good surface for baseball. It doesn't look very nice and doesn't play well, but it thrives on compacted earth with poor drainage. That's exactly what we had.

Joe and his crew had done all they could. He was very innovative. He kept a map that showed where the drainage was the worst and he had installed little PVC pipes that drained straight down, so, when water pooled up, they would just pop the cap to let it drain. I'd never seen that before. The field was built on landfill. The soil was silty, and the water table was high. Everyone knew we needed a new field, but the team was up for sale, so a dramatic change like that was out of the question.

The John Henry Group purchased the Red Sox in 2002. I had great support and could get anything we needed to maintain the field, as long as I justified it. Eventually, the need for a new field was evident to everyone. One game in 2004 seemed to be the last straw. We got only about a quarter inch of rain, but the game was postponed because the old field wouldn't drain and was way too soft. The next day, it was about eighty-five degrees, not a cloud in the sky. We had a helicopter fly over the field for about four or five hours to circulate the air and accelerate evaporation. We put down about ten tons of non-colored calcined clay infield conditioner that is similar to kitty litter but is heated at a high temperature to soak up water quickly. It was still too wet to play. Ownership realized we needed a new field and made a commitment to it.

The field wasn't the only mess. Although I loved my job, and work helped reduce my symptoms at the ballpark, I wasn't getting any better. Almost from the beginning of my time at Fenway, I started having issues with both my physical and emotional health.

Since Fenway had no automatic irrigation system, we had to be careful when watering the field. The best time to water the grass is between 2:00 a.m. and 6:00 a.m. That way, the grass doesn't stay wet all night, which can create additional stress, making it susceptible to disease. But it wasn't practical to have staff on duty overnight to run the sprinkler system, so we'd do it in the morning after cutting the grass, and then check the condition of the field and provide extra water as needed by hand, and we always had to water the infield and foul territory with hoses.

One morning in May of 2001, my first season, I decided to water the foul area grass while my staff was on break. I hooked up four fifty-foot sections of heavy, one-inch hose in the visitor's dugout, then stretched them out down the foul line behind third base and started watering, working my way toward the grass area behind home plate. Once I got that watered, I put the hose over my left shoulder and pulled hard to get it in position to water the foul ground along the first base line. As soon as I pulled on the hose I got an intense pain around my belt line on my lower back. It shot down into my left leg and foot like a lightning bolt, doubling me up in pain so much I couldn't stand upright. When I tried to walk I couldn't lift my left foot. I actually dragged it on the ground. Not only did my back hurt, but my left hamstring and buttocks were in an intense cramp. I was almost crying but, at the same time, I almost laughed. Here was my dream job, and now this!

I somehow made it through the game before going to see the team doctor. He said, "Your back is fucked, and you need to see a specialist right away. You need to get an MRI to start figuring out what's damaged."

The back specialist ordered the MRI, but I was in such pain I needed help to lie down. Afterwards, as the technician was helping me off the table, I asked him what he'd seen. He explained that he wasn't allowed to discuss it, but said, "I'll tell you this. I've done four thousand MRIs and your herniated disk is the biggest I've ever seen."

The doctor wanted me to have immediate surgery. He said I risked permanent nerve damage and warned me that, if I stumbled and fell, it might ruin my knee replacement. This was the first week of May, and I'd only been on the job a few months. I managed to make it to mid-July and had the surgery during the All-Star break.

It only helped for a short time. Soon the cramps and back pain returned. For the next few years, I'd toss and turn in bed trying to find a comfortable position, even using pillows under my legs and back. Nothing worked. I couldn't get any relief. I tried all kinds of different beds, but none made much difference. All I could do was to get up in the middle of the night and go stretch out in our reclining chair. Even after I moved the recliner into the bedroom several years later, I still felt guilty not being able to sleep in bed with Denise and be able to reach out and hug her. The feelings of guilt ate me up inside, and the added back pain only made falling asleep and my other PTSD symptoms worse.

But there were still many good memories. I always treasured the days when the girls would help me at work. The team was out of town on Saturday in late May and my ten-year-old daughter asked if she could come to work with me. I told her I'd love that. She asked what we would be doing at work and I said I was going to lay out the zeros that were in the mowing pattern for the hundredth anniversary of the Red Sox franchise. I asked if she wanted to help measure and lay those out and she excitedly said yes. I thought that, afterwards, while I was making the pattern with a walk-behind greens mower, she could water the foul territory. She had a better idea. "How about you hand water while I create the mowing pattern?" she asked. She had seen me use the mower before and had paid attention. I said I thought that was a fun idea. So we went and got the walk-behind mower and brought it out into place. I gave her a few tips about how to get started and she was a natural, rolling in the pattern with the roller that was on the mower. She even ended up creating the base-balls in the pattern while I proudly watched from the foul area while hand-watering the grass. I was proud and impressed. I just wish we had more of those moments together.

I hadn't learned to communicate any better; I was worried about being judged, and then I'd judge myself for not handling the situation right, for not saying or doing the right thing. I'd always been a light drinker, a social drinker but, in Milwaukee, there were times I drank too much at home. I had gotten into a routine of coming home after work and drinking a few rum and cokes, not to get drunk, but because I thought it helped me sleep. But, after Terry died, I realized that it was making me feel worse, so I stopped for a couple years. In 2002, however, my PTSD symptoms exploded and I started drinking again to help me sleep. I skipped the liquor and drank beer, telling myself that it wasn't really drinking because it was "only" beer. But I couldn't fool myself. And then I'd judge myself for drinking beer, and feel bad about that, and drink even more beer. I'd go to the store and it was like I had an angel on one shoulder saying, "You shouldn't be doing this. You don't need that," and I had a devil on the other shoulder saying, "Go ahead, buy the beer. You're gonna sleep better." Sometimes I'd stand in line and feel so guilty I'd put the beer back and drive home, then get mad at myself for not buying beer if I had more nightmares that night.

The drinking never really stopped the nightmares or the pain. I was just reaching out blindly, willing to try almost anything that I thought might help. After a while, it was more about drinking than the nightmares or sleep. It's funny how you can trick yourself. That's one of the reasons so many PTSD victims end up with substance abuse or addiction problems, trying to self-medicate and find their own solutions to problems that are bigger than what they can deal with alone. When those solutions fail to work, you feel even worse, and now have one more problem to deal with, one more reason to beat yourself up.

During the season, I was busy, although anniversaries of traumatic events could be tough. But, most of the time, I just worked and drank only sporadically, only when the team was out of town and after I arrived home earlier in the day. But I never drove while drinking, or drank while I was at work, or mixed pain medication with alcohol. I was afraid of what that might do, and if the pain was so bad that I had to take medication, I wouldn't drink at all that night or the next day. I never went out to bars. I did all my drinking at home, after work. But, in the offseason, where, all of a sudden,

I was working only a forty-hour week and had more down time, I drank even more.

In the offseason, I quickly fell into a routine. I'd come home, eat dinner with Denise and the girls, pretend everything was fine, then go into the basement, watch TV, and drink beer. Over time, I built up a tolerance, and usually ended up drinking eight or ten beers a night. I'd buy a thirty-pack and try to make sure I got four days out of it, and there were times I would leave two beers in it just, so I could say it made it to four days. But then I'd go out and buy another thirty-pack and start on that. I'd just do whatever I could to get away. Due to the alcohol and the medication I was taking and late-night snacks after waking from nightmares, I gained a tremendous amount of weight, eventually almost doubling my weight in school, up to about 350 pounds. That didn't help my pain or make me feel any better about myself either. The irony is that all this was taking place during one of the most exciting periods in Red Sox history, when they finally broke through and won the World Series in 2004, and during one of the most exciting times in my professional career.

One year before, on Saturday, October 4, 2003, I had my first opportunity after nineteen years in the Major Leagues to work a playoff game. This was a day I had dreamed of. It wasn't quite the same as being a player, but it was still a big deal. The air in Fenway was electric for the game against the Oakland A's, but the weather was less than ideal. It was a cool sixty degrees with heavy drizzle most of the day. After the tarp came off the infield, we had only thirty minutes to prepare for the game, but everything was going well. I was inspecting the infield when my cell phone rang. On the line was a Red Sox executive. "Come to Grady's office immediately!" he barked, and then hung up. My heart pounded in my throat. Why did I have to go to manager Grady Little's office? Was there a requirement for playoff games that I didn't know about? I went directly to the Red Sox dugout, through the runway, and up the steps to the clubhouse. I paused before opening the door to collect my thoughts and take a deep breath.

There stood Mr. Selig, the former owner of the Brewers and my old boss in Milwaukee, then serving as the Commissioner of Major League Baseball. He greeted me with a smile and a big hug saying, "I wanted to be sure to say hello when I was here. I know we have a chance of some rain during these games, but we couldn't be in better hands than with you. We dealt with a lot of rain, snow, fog, and even floods together in Milwaukee. You were always prepared for all of it." Then he asked about my family and said he hoped I enjoyed the playoffs. It was an incredibly kind gesture from a very kind man who I deeply respect.

Unfortunately, the Red Sox did not make it to the World Series in 2003. However, the day after the Red Sox swept the Cardinals to win the 2004 World Series, I received a call on my cell phone. Once again, it was Mr. Selig. "Congratulations, David!" he said. "You earned this opportunity through all of your hard work. I hope you really enjoy the moment." I could hardly believe the Commissioner thought to call me with so much else going on. If not for his confidence in me, I never would have had the chance to earn the opportunity to work behind the scenes of a World Series and receive a ring. Mr. Selig is one of my favorite people I have had the honor to meet in Major League Baseball.

There are many others. Hall of Famer Jim Rice has always been great to me, as was Nomar Garciaparra, the team's shortstop when I went to work in Boston. At first, however, he almost got me in trouble, although it wasn't his fault. Because of the loss of range of motion in my right knee, I have had to "one-foot it" up and down steps since 1981. I always go down steps one at a time, right foot first, move my left foot down beside it, repeating again and again, until I'm at the bottom of the flight. Early in the 2001 season, I was making my way down the dugout steps before the game when Manager Grady Little startled me. He yelled out, "What the hell are you doing? That is not funny. Nomar will be mad that you are making fun of him and I don't like it either!"

I was puzzled. "I have no idea what you're talking about."

"You walked down the steps exactly like Nomar," he said.

"I am not imitating anyone," I replied. Then I understood. Nomar had all sorts of routines and superstitions and one of them involved going down steps one at a time. I explained that I didn't have flexibility in my knee to walk down steps any other way, and I may have showed him my big scars as proof. Little understood. Problem solved.

Right after I had my back surgery, I got a call the next morning that Nomar wanted to work out the next day and to make sure the field was ready for him. He'd been out with an injury and was preparing to come back after the All-Star break. So, even though I'd just had surgery, I went into the park. At the time, then-Red Sox manager Jimy Williams wanted the infield grass cut high, three and a half inches, to slow down the ball to give his other infielders more time. It was so high that you could hear the ball as it scooted through the grass and, after we covered the field, we'd actually have to fluff it up, otherwise it looked matted.

After Nomar finished working out, he came over to me and said, "Dave, man, what's up with the infield grass?"

I said, "What do you mean, the height?"

"Yeah, it is, like, really high! I'm used to, like, an inch high. How high is it?"

"Three and a half inches."

"Man, I'm gonna be back after the All-Star break. Is there any way you could put it down to an inch tomorrow, so I can get used to the field again?" he asked.

I said, "Sure." We did what we could to keep the players happy.

My job was to make it work. A basic rule of thumb in regard to mowing grass is that you never want to mow off much more than one third of the grass at a time, because that stresses it. Well, we had to rush it and get it down to an inch in two days. The grass became stressed and turned neon yellow. I had to dye it green. When Nomar came out the next day he said, "Hey, thanks. Looks great."

Moments like that are what kept me at the ballpark. That, and the fear of going home and being alone with my thoughts. Keeping busy kept me going.

In the offseason after the 2004 World Championship, we began work on the new field. I was thrilled, not just because it would be a challenge, but because it would keep me at the ballpark. Not that I always stayed away from home but, when I was feeling better, I wanted to be home to be the best husband and father I could. I knew the more time I was home, the more time I might spend drinking to help with my pain and my sleep.

There was an incredible amount of planning to do, from engineering the field and doing water table studies, planning for irrigation, everything. We planned to remove the entire field that had been in place since 1934, all the sod and all the soil, and rebuild it from scratch. We brought in Roger Bossard, the White Sox groundskeeper who is considered the expert at constructing a new field. He had already installed more than a dozen, almost every recent new park in the majors, and had been my mentor for many years.

One of the things we knew we had to do was remove the eighteen-inch crown in the middle of the field, as it would no longer be necessary for drainage. As soon as the press heard that, I started getting angry calls. Everyone thought we were lowering the field everywhere, and that would change the height of the Green Monster, making it a foot taller. That was considered sacrilegious. Every Red Sox fan knew the wall was thirty-seven feet high and they wanted it to stay that way. People were asking, "What's this new guy think he's doing?"

That's not what we were doing. Yes, we were removing the crown, but then we were building the field back up and making it almost level. The new field would meet at the base of the Green Monster and all walls as before. It would be the same height but, instead of about a foot and a half of compacted dirt, we were putting in three inches of pea gravel and then nine inches of sand with a drainage system at fifteen-foot centers in a herringbone pattern. It drains better than the soil, creates a stronger root system, and the result is far safer and more playable that the old soil that had been in place for so long.

Before that, after skimming the old field off, we put in an automatic watering system with retractable irrigation heads. Everything was done to the strictest specs possible. We used laser levels while grading, and the end result is that centerfield is now flat. There's just a slight crown in right and left, and a bit of a slope in foul ground so our drain lines don't sit under the water table. Years ago, the area around Fenway was swampy, and the water table in that part of Boston is still affected by the tides. On the old field, the highest point had been in the infield, but now it's as flat as a pool table.

When we dug up the old field, we were curious about what we might find. Other than a few old medicine and ink bottles and the concrete footing for the goal posts when the Patriots played at Fenway, we didn't find much. The club sold the old sod to fans. People transplanted it in their lawns and even in graveyards. That's a Sox fan for you. Now Fenway grass is all over New England.

The new field was easier to work with, but it's also a more complicated process, because there are more variables we can monitor more closely and adjust. And I can track the weather better than ever too. The weather report is usually the first thing I check when I wake up and the last thing I check at night. The weather dictates so much of what we do—not only what jobs we're trying to accomplish but staffing. Nobody can water like Mother Nature but, when we do supplement watering, we're cautious, and make use of moisture sensors and temperature sensors throughout this field. We also use hand moisture meters. It's amazing how much we can monitor. Most homeowners use way too much water and way too much fertilizer. They think if a little bit's good, twice as much is going to be better, but they are only hurting their lawns and hurting the environment.

Keeping the field maintained takes time and attention. We usually start between 5:00 and 8:00 a.m., depending on the weather and what else is going on at the park. I'm so proud of my co-workers and staff. Four of us work full-time all year, then we have a seasonal staff of about fifty people, but all fifty are never working at the same time. We spread the staff shifts out, because the work can be all-consuming during the season.

When Mr. Mooney was in charge, he was very protective of the grass, and the Red Sox rarely held any events on the field. But, under the John Henry Group, an important part of our job became helping the club make the field available for charities, fundraisers, corporate functions, and special events like concerts to winter events like football, hockey, skiing, and snowboarding. One of the best parts of our job is to help people create memories. On some days, that means three shifts of the grounds crew staff, just to keep the field as safe, playable, and good-looking as possible. It's important to us that, when you go to Fenway Park for a game, you can never tell what took place on the field the previous day, or even earlier that afternoon.

Despite the success the team was having on the field and all the work we had done, no one really knew how I was feeling inside. It just kept getting worse emotionally and, over time, my back pain returned. I was miserable. In public, I just tried to put up a front, tried to be the positive guy, tried to be the happy guy, tried to be the life of the party. Anything to try to make people not notice what a mess I was.

In April of 2006, my back was hurt again while working on the bullpen mound and I had to have a two-level fusion of my vertebra. I had the surgery in July and was unable to work for a few weeks. Being away from the ballpark, combined with some painful anniversaries led my world to spin out of control again from my physical pain and PTSD symptoms. After surgery, I needed pain medication just to get through the day, and one of the side effects was fatigue. I was already exhausted from working long hours and not sleeping due to nightmares and, the first week after returning to work from surgery, I twice fell asleep driving home from night games. Each time, my car drifted off the road when I was only a few miles from home. Fortunately, both times, I was jolted awake by the sound of my tires on the gravel at the edge of the pavement. I had just enough time to steer the car back onto the road to avoid crashing into a tree. It scared the hell out of me. Each time, I got out of the car, paced back and forth, trying to calm down and wake up at the same time. Then I drove home the remaining five minutes with the windows wide open, hoping that would keep me from falling asleep, and called my friend Jason to talk to me and help keep me awake till I got home.

I felt like I was playing Russian roulette. I was terrified of falling asleep again, wrecking my car, and possibly hurting someone. I knew I couldn't live with myself if that happened. I called my doctor and said I couldn't take that medicine anymore. He agreed that I should stop taking the medication, but I would need to be weaned off of it gradually. I wasn't as tired, but I suffered from terrible pain once I was off the medicine. Too often, my answer was alcohol.

One evening in July, I was downstairs drinking, sitting in a recliner, watching TV when Denise came down to speak with me. She wasn't loud, and she wasn't angry, but she was direct and serious. She said she wished I would stop drinking because it was worrying her and, more importantly, worrying the girls. She explained that I wasn't the same person when I drank even though I thought I was. She said by going downstairs and drinking I was separating myself from them. I was shocked; it hit me like a lightning bolt and broke my heart. I'd always thought I was a "happy drinker" and wasn't hurting anyone. I didn't even think I was hurting myself. I just hoped it would help me sleep so I could function well the following day. I thought I could handle the alcohol and had done everything I could to protect my family. But I now realized I had let down the most important people in my life. I was so wrapped up in my own world of emotional and physical pain that I had become oblivious to their feelings. When she said I was worrying her "and, more importantly, our girls," it grabbed my attention like never before. I knew then that I couldn't continue drinking. Looking back, I regret that I missed many opportunities to be a better dad. I was furious at myself. I had tried my best to not burden them with the pain and turmoil I was going through, and I had failed horribly. It broke my heart.

I stopped drinking that day, cold turkey, and have not had a drink since. I couldn't fix the pain I had already caused my family, but I was going to try to be a better husband and father.

It was an important step in my recovery. Soon, I would take another one.

Chapter 13

Although I had stopped drinking, my physical pain increased throughout the rest of the 2006 baseball season. I was barely getting through the day. I knew I couldn't keep going on. Nearly every waking moment was dominated by pain and fear. By the end of the season, I knew I had to do something. Although I was still too afraid to talk about my emotions, I knew I had to address the physical pain. I made a deal with myself. Even though I felt weak for even considering it, I decided to ask for help. I told myself that, if that worked, if that was successful and my pain became manageable, that perhaps my internal torment would lessen. At least, that's what I hoped and prayed for.

Twenty-seven separate surgeries had taken a toll on my body and on my soul. I was disappointed in myself for not being able to deal with the pain. But it had finally come to the point that the pain was worse than the shame I felt. That had taken twenty-five long years.

I had a heart-to-heart conversation with Denise about how miserable the chronic pain was making me. It dominated my life. It didn't matter that I couldn't go down stairs two at a time, or that I had slept in a recliner for over a year because I couldn't find a comfortable position in bed because of my back. The problem was not what I could or couldn't do, it was that the pain had become so debilitating that it was beginning not to matter what I did at all. Combined with my PTSD symptoms, it was so overwhelming, so incapacitating that it took all my energy to try to ignore it. I almost couldn't think about anything or anyone else. The pain was always there, always pulling at me, distracting me, trying to take me away. I had battled it for as long as I could. I needed help. I could not continue my battle alone.

Although I had feared Denise's reaction, and feared that she would judge me, from the first moment I opened my mouth, she was supportive. At some level, she knew, but she had also known me well enough to know that, unless I reached out for help myself, I was unlikely to accept it. She committed herself to helping me in any way she could. I look back now and wonder how I could have ever thought she would react in any other way.

I thought back to my "one-base-at-a-time" philosophy. That was how I had always dealt successfully with physical therapy and that was how I decided I would approach this issue, as a series of small steps and accomplishments. I had always thought of pain as something I should be able to control on my own. I realize now just how inadequate that approach was. It was like I had been trying to keep the grass cut at Fenway Park with a pair of scissors. My pain had been increasing for years, becoming ever more draining, and there was simply no way for me to keep up. It was like a disease, something that was happening to me. Willpower was not enough.

Denise insisted I contact my doctor that day. I called my incredible primary care physician and told him that I needed help with my pain and was surprised that he was so supportive and non-judgmental. He referred me to a pain specialist who could design an all-encompassing pain management program. I hadn't even known there was such a thing as a pain management specialist and have since learned that more people suffer from chronic pain than cancer. I had focused so much on work and suppressing my reactions to pain, that I never knew there were alternatives. I had no idea how many other people suffered from debilitating, chronic pain for a wide variety of causes and that, in the last few decades, the medical community had made great strides in treatment. It wasn't just, "Here, take this pill and you'll feel better."

I started working with the Massachusetts General Hospital Pain Clinic and spent nearly a week in the hospital so they could do a full evaluation—what kind of pain I was experiencing, how bad, where, and how often. I underwent all sorts of neurological tests and other evaluations, so the doctors could get the clearest picture possible of what I was dealing with. Only then would they know how to proceed. Much of this process required my feedback, honest and complete answers to their questions. That was incredibly difficult for me to do because I had to finally be honest about how badly I was hurting. I also had to trust the doctors. Ever since the incident in PT, I had a deep distrust of medical professionals. They had to earn my confidence over time, and I was still keeping my PTSD symptoms a secret. I had spent my whole adult life building this fiction that I was the guy who didn't complain and "just got it done." Now I had to open up. It wasn't easy. For the past twenty-five years I had always underestimated my pain. If I was asked what my pain level was on a scale of 1-10, even though there were many times it was a 10, I might only say 2 or 3 or 4. In some instances, by underreporting my pain, I had needlessly suffered. Had I been honest, I may have received much better pain treatment from the beginning. But it was still hard. My first impulse was always to make it sound better than it really was, and to say that treatments worked better than they really did. I know now that honest communication is absolutely essential for doctors to develop a proper pain management treatment plan. It was like a parent talking to a toddler—if a child doesn't tell you what hurts, how can you help? For years, part of me had blamed the doctors for my pain when, in fact, they had only been responding to the incomplete picture I had given them. I think my PTSD can be blamed for some of that as well. It made me pretty adept at fooling people, particularly myself.

Everyone at Mass General, from the nurses to the technicians to the doctors, was incredibly supportive. They dealt with this all the time. They didn't blame me for being in pain. They only wanted to help.

I had a complicated case. My pain wasn't caused by a single event or trauma, but by many. Over the years, my knee and back injuries had put all sorts of abnormal stresses on my body. Some muscles and bones were overburdened, and I had some nerve damage and alignment issues. It was hard to be certain that solving one problem might not create another one. Treating me for pain was sort of like playing "Whack-a-Mole." It was hard to keep all the pain under control at the same time, and a challenge to realize how one treatment might impact another.

After being released from the hospital, I saw a pain specialist regularly. Over time, my doctors developed a multi-level attack on my pain. Several varieties of medication were eventually prescribed, including drugs to address pain, nerve sensitivity, anti-inflammatories, and muscle relaxers.

I never found any pain medication to be the least bit enjoyable or euphoric—I never took any pleasure from them whatsoever. I only took prescribed medicine as directed by my doctors. Even those that provided relief often caused side effects that were problematic, ranging from dizziness to headaches, constipation, and other unpleasant reactions. Speaking for myself, I cannot understand using pain medication for recreational purposes.

Prescription medication was only a partial solution, one that never really addressed the underlying issues. I worked with the doctors to try a wide variety of other treatments that, at times, included cortisone shots, trigger point injections, radiofrequency lesion procedures, transcutaneous electrical nerve stimulation, acupuncture, massage, ice, heat, saunas, hot water whirlpool treatments, stretching, swim therapy, relaxation exercises, physical therapy, occupational therapy, biofeedback, and the implantation of an electrical spinal cord stimulator. If that sounds like the doctors were trying everything to see what worked best, well, in a way they were. It was important for me to realize that there was never going to be a single "magic bullet" that would cure me of my pain, instantaneously and forever. In all likelihood, it would always have to include a multitude of approaches.

Massage, acupuncture, even biofeedback all helped and, cumulatively, they added up. I thought the biofeedback and relaxation techniques were fascinating. The doctor would have me sit in a recliner hooked up to all these monitors, while I looked at a computer screen with a picture of a stream on it. As he gently spoke and gave me instructions, I learned to relax and control my heart rate. As it went lower, planks would appear on the screen and begin to build a bridge. As I got better at relaxing, I eventually built a bridge the entire way across. I thought that was fascinating and helpful. At the end, my heart rate and breathing would be way down, and there was this bridge over the stream, a small measure of progress, one step at a time.

I was also treated with radio frequency, which burned the end of a nerve that caused pain. That could provide three to six months of relief. The idea was that, by the time the nerve grew back, the underlying cause could be treated without causing pain. I had terrible muscle spasms and cramps, and Botox was injected directly into muscle knots, sometimes providing almost instant relief. My doctor, for much of this time, was absolutely incredible. She had a great bedside manner and really earned my trust. I tried everything she suggested.

Other treatments were more dramatic. The spinal cord stimulator has been particularly effective—and frustrating. The stimulator is a small electronic device with a wire that is threaded into your spine. It sends an electric signal to the brain that is supposed to inter-rupt the pain signal. When the doctors told me I was a candidate, although the device is normally implanted under the skin, at first, they kept it outside my body for a two-day trial, with only the wire going into my spine. I'll never forget the first time they turned it on. Instantly, for the first time since I was struck by a car at that McDonald's in 1991, my knee pain dropped by more than half, even though it was designed to ease pain in my left lower back. I smiled and turned to Denise and started to tear up, because the pain in my knee was so reduced. I hadn't thought that would ever happen.

A short time later, I had the device implanted, and it worked great for a few months, then the wire somehow moved, and the impulses started affecting other parts of my body. They opened me up and did an adjustment and got it working correctly again but, on a rainy day at Fenway, while walking down the ramp by my office, I slipped. I caught myself before I fell, but my left buttock, right where the stimulator was implanted, slammed against the corner of a handrail. They had to take it out. They tried another one, but it never worked right. I'd bend down to pick up a sunflower seed or something and it would shock the hell out of me, so they took that one out too. A few years later, we tried another stimulator, with an internal accelerometer, which acts kind of like a gyroscope that was more involved, a sixteen-electrode paddle. But, as the surgery for the implant healed, scar tissue caused the wire to shift. Instead of bringing relief to my left side, it began affecting my right side. We were just about ready to have it taken out when I fell and broke my hip. Incredibly, purely by chance, the stimulator helped with my hip pain. Any relief was better than none, so we left it in.

At times, pain management was frustrating and time consuming but, at the same time, I was getting some relief and I knew the process wasn't futile. Physically, that made a huge difference for me. But the rest of me was just getting worse. Although Denise has since told me I would never have won an Oscar for my ability to act like nothing was going on inside me, she still had no idea exactly how bad it was or how hard I worked to prevent her from knowing the full extent of my troubles. If she did, I was certain she would leave me, and I would lose her and the girls.

Nevertheless, she knew of my turmoil. She had lived with my mood swings, irritability, restlessness, extreme sensitivity, and screaming nightmares. Memories of the accidents, the PT incident, and my brother's sudden death didn't always affect me during the day, but nights were increasingly torturous. There were times that, as soon as I woke up and started my day, I would begin to stress out and worry about the nightmares I had just experienced. By the afternoon, that would combine with and trigger flashbacks of past traumas, leaving me with even more anxiety about going to sleep. At some point every evening, a dread would set in. I knew the terrible experience that awaited me. At least my other symptoms came and went—sometimes I could go a day or two without a serious flashback. But, as the sun went down, my fear grew. As evening approached, a crippling anxiety would set off cold sweats, heart palpitations, raised blood pressure, even migraine headaches.

Night after night, I would sit watching TV before drifting off sometime after midnight, hoping that, if I screamed and woke Denise and the girls, I could blame it on the TV. Then came the nightmares, three-dimensional, high-definition, surround-sound horror movies of each and every traumatic incident in excruciating detail, so vivid I could feel, hear, taste, touch, and smell every aspect.

Every night, after I drifted off, I would hear a car engine revving and tires squealing. I would see a car speeding at me and try to flee, but my feet were cemented in the ground. I never got away. The car lights would close in on me. Then I'd feel the impact, the warm bumper and grill crash against my leg, my body flying through the air. Sometimes I'd feel my face making contact with the windshield, the only experience in the dreams that did not actually happen. Then I'd hear the glass door of the McDonald's shatter, feel the heat of the engine on my face and smell the exhaust as I was pinned against the wall. I'd push at the car with all my might, but it felt white-hot and I'd reflexively pull away and check for burns, then see the photographer's camera flashing as I lay in pain, helpless. Faces would flash before my eyes—the women at McDonald's, the physical therapist, the deranged woman from County Stadium laughing at me. I'd try to wake up but couldn't. The dream was a flood I was powerless to stop. I'd feel the weights shift on my leg, hear my ligaments tear and pop, and reach out too late to keep my leg from falling. I'd see Terry in his casket, see my leg with a raw open incision, feel the pain from my knee exploding and scream and scream and scream.

I'd wake up in a panic, gasping for air, my ears ringing, and look for Denise, to see if I'd woken her. Then I'd check on the girls for the same reason. If I had woken them up, I'd feel guilty and furious with myself for letting my nightmares disrupt their lives. If I hadn't, I was simply afraid I would the next time. Then I'd lay back down, my sheets often soaked in sweat, my heart racing, petrified, exhausted, muscles cramping and twitching like I was possessed, my body throbbing in pain, my head pounding, knowing I needed to sleep, exhausted, but not wanting to, then lying awake, hearing my heart, counting my breaths, staring into space, drifting off...and then, if I fell back asleep, many times, it would start all over again. A second time, a third, a fourth. Every. Single. Night.

I thought I was condemned to live this way for the rest of my life. I believed there was no way to stop it. Then, on September 23, 2010, Terry's birthday, incidentally, nearly twenty-nine years after being struck by the car at McDonald's, I learned this was not the case.

I was laying on the table of my acupuncturist. I usually tried to find something enjoyable to read during treatment, *Reader's Digest*, if I could, because I always enjoyed the regular features like "Laughter is the Best Medicine." That's how I got through my days, putting on the happy face, laughing and joking. There wasn't a copy available, however, so I opted for a copy of *Smithsonian Magazine*, flipping through the pages until I came across a short article titled "The Pathway Home Makes Inroads Treating PTSD" by Robert Poole.

Cacky was studying Holistic Psychology and Art Therapy at Lesley College in Cambridge, Massachusetts. She wanted to be a psychologist and was interested in working with people who had experienced trauma, like many of our soldiers who had returned from the Middle East. In fact, she was already interning with the Home Base program at Mass General. She may have been their very first intern.

I started to read the article mainly because she was interested in the subject, thinking I would talk with her about it the next time I saw her. Of course, I knew what PTSD was...or I thought I did. It was a problem soldiers sometimes had due to their experience in war.

I started reading.

They went off to war brimming with confidence and eager for the fight in Iraq and Afghanistan. They returned, many of them, showing no visible wounds but utterly transformed by combat—with symptoms of involuntary trembling, irritability, restlessness, depression, nightmares, flashbacks, insomnia, emotional numbness, sensitivity to noise, and, all too often, a tendency to seek relief in alcohol, drugs or suicide.

Wait a minute. That felt familiar.

I read it again, this time more closely. As I did, I started ticking off the symptoms that had haunted me for almost thirty years. *Involuntary trembling?* Sometimes. *Irritability?* Often. *Restlessness?* Yes. *Depression?* Absolutely. *Nightmares?* Always. *Insomnia?* Definitely. *Emotional numbness?* Yes. *Sensitivity to noise?* Yes! *A tendency to seek relief in alcohol?* I HAD!

With each affirmative response, it began to dawn on me, first slowly, but then in a rushing flood. Apart from drugs and suicide, at one time or another, I had experienced every single symptom cited. And not just once in a while, but almost all the time, virtually every day, except for the drinking. *Could I have PTSD? Was that possible?* I read on. Every word felt like a hammer strike breaking a dam.

"There's no compassion. I felt constantly ridiculed," said one victim, adding that he had marriage difficulties and a drinking problem that was ineffective at dealing with his symptoms. That was me, or had been, or could have been. There was more. A picture accompanied the article, which focused on the treatment facility in California. It showed several veterans sitting together in a restaurant. They looked happy. "I came here thinking it was my last option. I would be dead if I didn't have this program," one vet who had PTSD since 2004 was quoted as saying. But then it said that he had ended treatment in less than a year and had just moved into a house with his new wife. "I know I'm going to be OK," he said. He had suffered from PTSD for years. He had gotten treatment. He was feeling better. He knew he was going to be OK. He didn't just hope so. He *knew*.

I read on about the program, about the treatment plan. It seemed to work a lot like pain management. They tried different things, realizing each person's experience was unique. Counseling, yoga, acupuncture, group therapy all played a part in recovery. Some patients were young, only a year or two out of battle. Some were as old as I was and had suffered for years.

"We give them the tools to realize when they're spinning and need to stop," said one of the people who worked there. "They learn to modulate their emotions." All of them were getting better.

That first paragraph, the list of symptoms, by itself, was overwhelming. As I read it over and over, I recognized myself for the first time. I wasn't "different." I wasn't just "messed up." There was something wrong with me, something that many others had, and something that could successfully be treated.

Tears ran down my face. Could I finally have a name for the turmoil I'd felt since July 10, 1981? I trembled. I could actually feel what the article was describing. But I had always thought PTSD was a condition only soldiers who had dealt with the horrors of war could have. Could I really be suffering from the same disorder? What would it mean in my life and to my family if I did have PTSD? What would it mean if there was actually an effective treatment?

What I did know, clearly, was that what I had been doing for the last twenty-nine years wasn't working. I was scared, but I knew I needed to learn more about what PTSD was and how it was treated. And I had to find out now. In order to do that, I had to talk about it. I had to tell Denise. I had been practicing that speech for twenty-nine years. Now it was finally time to say the words to her out loud. I owed it to my family. I owed it to myself.

Chapter 14

*A*s I sat there staring at the article in my hands, waves of emotion surged through my body. There was a lot of fear but there was something else—hope. For the first time ever, I thought I might have some idea about what was wrong with me, that there may be a way to stop the nightmares and panic attacks, and that I might finally become the husband and father I wanted to be.

Prior to that moment, it had never occurred to me that I might have PTSD. No one had ever mentioned the possibility, and I had never before connected the dots myself. The description of the symptoms and my own experience were so clear and direct that it became obvious to me that I was suffering from PTSD too.

I pulled it together for the acupuncture session, laying there the entire time thinking about the article, trying to process what I just learned, and steeling myself to talk to Denise.

When the appointment was through, I was afraid to ask if I could take the magazine with me. I'm sure it would have been all right but, at that moment, I was too emotionally fragile and could barely talk. Before I left—and I'm embarrassed to say this—I tore out the part of the article that listed the symptoms because I wanted to be sure

I could explain them all to Denise. I didn't want to forget anything. It was only about an inch long, but I tucked it into my pocket like it was the most valuable item on earth. I've since felt guilty about it, worrying that I may have deprived someone else of the opportunity of becoming enlightened in the way that I did.

I've often thought back to the instant when I first picked up the magazine, and how fortunate and lucky that was. What if another magazine had caught my eye? What if I had missed the article? But, then again, what if those two women back in 1981 had decided to go to a Burger King instead of McDonald's, or what if I hadn't left my wallet in the car? Maybe I'd have made it as a major league pitcher. But maybe I never would have met Denise or had two such wonderful children. You can drive yourself crazy asking questions like that. Somehow, someway, all things happen for a purpose. I know this did.

I got in the car and, for the millionth time, rehearsed what I was going to say. But, whereas before, I had always struggled with the idea that, if I didn't explain it all in precisely the right way, she might think I was crazy and either tell me she wanted a divorce or to just suck it up and get over it, this time I knew I had to get past that anxiety. I had to tell her. I'd been living a secret life all these years and, no matter how scared I was of the stigma of asking for psychological help, I had to do it.

When I got home, I was almost shaking. Denise was in the bedroom. I looked at her, and with my lower lip trembling, I said, "Honey, we have to talk." She looked up. Due to the constant pain in my body, I often stand instead of sitting, but I was so nervous, so shaky, that I was afraid I might pass out. My heart was beating a thousand times a minute and I could hardly catch my breath. So I sat down, inhaled deeply, and started talking.

I don't remember the exact words, but I told her about the article, all the things I experienced, the flashbacks, panic attacks, the triggers and nightmares, the list of symptoms and how I had almost every one. I went right down the list. I told her how this had been going on for years, since before we had even met, and how brokenhearted I was to have put her and the girls through so much.

"I think I have PTSD."

I was frightened and nervous. I was crying. I was shaking. This was way more difficult than anything I had ever experienced before. Staying closed had been hard enough but opening up was even more difficult.

I told her that I actively had or had experienced ten of the twelve symptoms. I told her that I didn't just have the symptoms sometimes, but all the time and that, later that night, I would go to bed and have nightmares, just like I had every night for the past twenty-nine years. This was as certain as the sun coming up. It hung over me every day.

I don't remember exactly what she said, but everything I had feared might happen did not happen. Denise did not run away. She didn't reject or judge me, as I feared for all those years. She listened. The more I talked, the easier it became. She didn't ask to be alone to process things and she never made me more self-conscious than I already was. She just listened, showing as much compassion and understanding as any therapist with decades of training and experience.

Then, as I paused and groped for words to help explain, she said, "Honey, let's do this together. You are not alone. I'm here for you." What beautiful words to hear.

She reminded me that I had many friends, that we knew many people at Mass General through the pain management program, that there were people we could reach out to for advice, who could tell us where to turn. There were, she said, many people willing to help.

We talked for a long time. I told her as much as I could think of and she understood it all. She was already looking ahead, and she was getting me to do the same. She let me know that, from this moment forward, I could start to get better, and that she would be with me the entire time. Talking through my private hell was one of the hardest things I've ever had to do, but her response made it so much easier. I cannot give her enough credit. There was not a moment that she wavered, not a second during the entire conversation that she was anything less than supportive. She didn't press or push. I was so fragile at that moment that the smallest thing—a raised eyebrow, the wrong tone of voice—would have shut me down. I would have been crushed. It would have confirmed everything I'd worried about for so long. None of that happened.

I still dreaded going to sleep that night, and I still experienced nightmares but, the next morning, we picked up the phone.

Comedian Lenny Clarke is a big Red Sox fan and is always helping the ballclub at various events. Back in 2004, as a gesture of thanks, Red Sox owner John Henry asked Lenny if there was anyone with the club he wanted to meet. Mr. Henry would arrange for Lenny to have lunch with them. I think he expected Lenny to ask to meet with one of the teams' big stars like Manny Ramirez, David Ortiz, Jason Varitek, or Johnny Damon. Lenny told him he wanted to meet me. I have to think Mr. Henry was shocked. As it turns out, Lenny is a "grass groupie." He's really into his lawn. Lenny being Lenny, he says, "I used to smoke it, but now I just mow it." We had a blast at lunch and immediately became great friends.

Now, Lenny put us in touch with a friend at Mass General who could help me get in to see some of the top people, the doctors who either don't accept new patients or are booked months in advance.

Thanks to Lenny and his friend, I was able to book an appointment with one of the most respected psychologists in the country.

The day I went in for my initial appointment, I was filled with trepidation. I'm not, in any way, famous but it always surprises me how many people recognize me around Boston. They'll recognize me from being at the ballpark. It's not unusual for someone to come up to me and say, "Hey, aren't you the groundskeeper at Fenway?" or for a stranger just to say, "Hi, Dave," and shake my hand. On this day, I did not want to be recognized. I kept looking over my shoulder and lowering my head.

The psychologist's office was like something you'd see in a movie. There was a couch and a few chairs. Everything was quiet. The doctor was pleasant and soft-spoken. But that didn't make it easy to open up. I had no problem telling him why I was there, how I had discovered the article and thought I had PTSD, but all I was really giving him were the facts, a thumbnail description of my life about as detailed as the back of a baseball card. I gave him the bullet points on my traumatic experiences, but I wasn't anywhere close to the point where I was willing to share the raw details of my inner world. I didn't want to bring up any emotion that might cause my voice to crack, my eyes to water, or send me into a flashback right in front of him, so I just kept things clinical.

The doctor was incredibly patient. He explained to me that PTSD was not, and never had been, solely the result of traumatic wartime experiences. All sorts of events can cause PTSD. One of the most common causes is car accidents, something first widely recognized in the 1997 book *After the Crash: Psychological Assessment and Treatment of Survivors of Motor Vehicle Accidents* by Edward Blanchard and Edward Hickling. A year after publication, the medical community agreed with their assessment and motor vehicle accidents were added as a potential cause of PTSD in the *Diagnostic and Statistical*

Manual of Mental Disorders. For many people, a car accident may well be the most traumatic experience of their lives. Not only can car accidents be physically traumatic, but many victims suffer alone for a number of minutes before receiving care, just as I did when pinned against the wall or laying on the warning track. It is during that window that victims feel the most vulnerable and when the triggers are formed, resulting in PTSD.

It probably didn't help me that I knew that this Doctor, who was very nice and professional, was also very expensive. He didn't take insurance. He only accepted cash, and his rate was about $400 an hour. The Red Sox pay me a very good salary, but that was out of reach, at least for a sustained period. I told him that the second time I saw him, and he was very understanding. He agreed to keep seeing me without charge until I found someone else through the hospital. He made it clear he wasn't concerned about the money, he just wanted me to get better. That was comforting.

It is important to understand, for anyone beginning PTSD treatment or any other kind of psychotherapy, that positive results are not instantaneous. Your first doctor and first method of treatment might not be ideal matches. Each case is unique, as is each doctor and each treatment protocol. A doctor who was perfect for me and the style of treatment that was effective in my case might not work for someone else. The process itself is progress. To that end, it's critical to give the process a chance and allow for the fact that you might have to change doctors or treatments. For someone just opening up and coming forward for the first time, this can be incredibly difficult to accept. Years before, I had seen a psychiatrist a single time and never returned. Fortunately, my more recent experience with pain management had taught me that there is no "one-size-fits-all" approach to medicine. It's like dieting or exercising. You can't lose all the weight or build all the muscle in a day or a week or a month.

The results are down the road and come from a commitment to the program. Although I didn't see my first doctor for long, he played an important role. He didn't push me away, and I didn't back down. He gave me the confidence to continue moving forward. He helped me take the first steps to where I am today and served as the bridge that led me to effective treatment.

After a few weeks, I was put in touch with a psychologist and her colleague. I felt comfortable with them from the beginning. They were both incredible people, with great bedside manner, easy to talk to, and exceptionally compassionate. That was important, because, at least initially, many of my sessions consisted of them gently asking questions and me doing my best to answer them, to provide some idea about the dimensions of my problem so she could begin to come up with a plan for treatment. She had to learn my history, why I was there, before gradually getting me to talk in more detail about what had happened and how it was still bothering me. I had to learn to be forthcoming, because I had spent years not telling the truth about my pain.

Whenever anyone asked how I was, my standard answer was, "I'm hanging in there." It was a non-answer but telling in its way. I didn't want to lie and say everything was super when it wasn't, but I also was never going to be blunt and say, "I didn't sleep last night because I have nightmares and life sucks right now." No one wants to hear that.

Denise and I told the girls that I was getting treatment right away. Once I realized I wasn't embarrassed about getting help, I felt I had to let them know. They understood. I was so proud of them. Kids are perceptive. They had known that there was something wrong with me, they just didn't know what. I actually think Cacky knew, or at least sensed what was wrong. It was just too coincidental that she was already interning with a PTSD program. I believe she recognized my symptoms before I did. When I told them, I made a promise that I was going to get help and would not quit, no matter how challenging the treatment was. They were a big reason I was doing this, to try to become the father that I wanted to be. They deserved that, and I knew I would not break my promise. It was too important.

Initially, I saw the therapist twice a week for about an hour, but then I stepped up and met doctors on Monday for an hour, and then an hour and a half on Friday.

Even though I'd brought my family into the loop, the Red Sox were not. Telling my family was one thing, but I was still scared of the stigma and embarrassed to tell anyone else. It was hard to see real progress at first. Although, today, I am proud to be a PTSD survivor, at the start of my journey, I was still frightened and embarrassed.

One thing that really surprised me when I started therapy, is the amount of time that nobody talks. As we spoke with one another and the doctor asked questions, or I tried to articulate what I was feeling, because it's so powerful and emotional, there were long stretches of silence as I searched for the right words while trying to contain the pain and the sorrow. Sometimes I just wasn't ready to talk. That was fine. They were so good at letting me take my time and not pressuring me to speak before I was ready to, allowing me to regain my composure, grab a tissue, or just walk around the room. Whatever it was, they knew how to lead me forward, so I didn't shut down, always saying the right things at the right time, asking the right question, or encouraging me by letting me know that what I was going through was normal, that I wasn't crazy. Everybody's symptoms are different, but a lot of them are similar, and it was reassuring to hear that I was not the only person going through this. For twenty-nine years, I thought I was.

This was the first time I had ever talked about any of this. It as in fits and starts and very difficult. Then, at a certain point, e asked, "Do you mind if we record everything we're doing?" e assured me I would have the only copy and explained that she anted me to take the recordings home and lsten to them on my vn, that it would begin to help desensitize me to the experience.

This was a kind of cognitive behavioral therapy, prolonged expo- re, specific to treating PTSD, and I was very fortunate because, th me, the first strategy we tried was effective. But that isn't ying it was instantaneous or easy. Because it was not. It was credibly difficult and painful. It wasn't like, "We're going to take re of everything all in one sitting," or, "We're going to cover all ose years at once." We began by going through my traumas indi- dually, breaking them down, one by one, in excruciating detail and ing through the same basic procedure with each.

We spent weeks going over the accident at McDonald's, talking out it in as much detail as I could recall. Over time, almost without alizing it, I became more comfortable speaking about it. After ch session, I would listen to a recording and go through it again. ch stage was painful. As I talked about McDonald's, I broke down tears repeatedly, many times, before I was finally able to speak out it without crying or having such a pronounced reaction. But, en I would listen to the recordings at home or while driving, it s like I was undergoing the initial therapy session a second time. was like starting over. I would cry and have a similar emotional sponse. Sometimes, it would be so powerful I would have to pull e car over to the side of the road. But that was the point. With ch retelling, over time, my reactions to the event would inspire s of an emotional reaction.

The doctors explained this all to me. The fact that I had an emo- onal reaction wasn't a sign of weakness. It was a sign of strength,

Just after my story became known, I met a woman who told me, "Your story is so powerful. My story is not that bad. My PTSD is nothing." She had experienced a fire in her house when she was a kid. To this day, if she sees fire, it petrifies her. It changes her demeanor and everything, bringing back memories of the incident. Everybody's PTSD is significant. There's no lesser or worse degree, whether your experience was stimulated by a car wreck, an IED, or a fire. After we talked, and I explained that to her, she was willing to see a doctor and started to feel better. She realized her PTSD was something important after all.

Oftentimes, we put on that false bravado, or think, "Oh, it's not that big a deal. It's not as bad as somebody else's." I've learned that, at whatever level something is bothering you, if you don't get it fixed, if you don't get it off your chest, chances are it's going to fester and evolve into something much worse, negatively impacting your life in significant ways. Everybody has their own self-defense mech- anisms. We sugarcoat it, we mask it, we do something else to try to forget. We have to learn not to. That's what therapy did for me.

There are many different kinds of treatment available today, but the first step is generally some kind of counseling to assess the symptoms and causes. From there, treatment can go off in many directions. Treatments generally begin with individual psycho- therapy, during which time the doctors and patient set goals for treatment and find a way to get there. This might include cognitive and behavioral processing, which entails exploring how a person thinks about a problem and responds to it affects the way they process it emotionally. It can also include various exposure thera- pies, which seeks to desensitize the individual to reminders of the event by a variety of methods, or even group therapy, where people find support among others with similar experiences, and find it easier to open up in such a setting.

I regard my experience as a teaching tool now and see it as my responsibility to let people know that they can feel better too, whether you're the toughest person or the smallest child. Anyone who suffers trauma needs help. Don't be discouraged if you don't gel with the first doctor or counselor you meet. There are many options out there. Find somebody else. Somebody's out there who can help you. There are so many different incredible treatments now. There's Somatic experiencing, and EMDR, Eye Movement Desensitization and Reprocessing, which is a technique that helps victims develop different coping mechanisms. When I visited the Home Base program at Mass General, I saw one treatment that makes use of virtual reality simulators. A patient sits in a chair wearing goggles and it's like they're back in Afghanistan. They can customize the experience. The seat rumbles and they can smell burning rubber and gun powder. It's amazing what they can do to help de-sensitize all those bare emotions. And new treatments are being developed and refined all the time. There are so many things out there for people that I didn't have any idea about.

Some patients use a combination of approaches or go from one kind of treatment to the next. Some supplement treatment with prescription medication. There is no "one-size-fits-all" approach, no "failure," just a long and potentially protracted search for the method that works best, what helps now, and continues to help on your path to recovery.

Most of the time, the first approach won't be effective. My doctor told me at the outset that it will get worse before it gets better. That was true. I wondered if I could handle it, but I refused to go back on my promise to my daughters. Undergoing therapy was like going though those knee manipulations. I had a lot of emotional scar tissue to work through. It was never easy, but I knew that it had to be done.

I realized early on that speaking about my trouble symptoms. The first day I met with my doctor, we w room with a chair in the corner. As I said before, I down, especially given what I was going through the back was badly bothering me. I even stand at meeting the doctor had asked me to sit, so I did. We started tal incident at McDonald's and it felt like the walls were me. Ever since that accident I have never felt comforta I started to have a flashback. All of a sudden, I wa pinned to the ground, fear and anxiety coursing throu could hear the car and smell the engine. I felt deeply sitting, and I said, "Excuse me, ma'am, but, if you d got to stand up. This is really uncomfortable for m corner, I feel like I'm back at McDonald's."

That was fine with her. As a result, she earned respect right away, because I realized she wasn't going knew then that I could be honest with her. I stood and the room till the episode passed. That was enormou because, in the past, whenever I experienced a fla people, I would just get up and find some excuse to l All she said was, "I want you to be comfortable." I wa would allow things to unfold at my own pace, and in frame. There was no hint of impatience or pressur was genuine. It wasn't just then, but every time. In o ings, we'd often start with a short computer survey a feeling. There were maybe ten questions, such as: "H now?" "How do you feel compared to last week?" safe?" Doctors know the process is stressful, and the sure you are not suicidal, that something more signifi bothering you because, if it is, they want you to speal to know. After taking the quiz, I would start talking.

a sign that I was beginning to live with the experience rather than bury it or push it away. In a way, I was finally having the kind of emotional response that had escaped me for so long, the kind of response I needed to go through, to admit that this had happened and that it had a significant impact on me, rather than pretending it hadn't.

After I became comfortable listening to my session, the doctors had me write the experiences down. I would go to therapy on Monday, and my assignment for the rest of the week would be to sit down and write it all out. You might think that would be easier, because I had already talked about the trauma so much. But it wasn't. It was another level of opening up, of re-experiencing the initial experience. I would sit at home in my recliner with a yellow legal pad and try to write. At first, it was almost like shorthand. I was just making notes, reacting, sketching almost, writing in fragments.

Writing about it made it seem like I'd never talked about it before, like I'd never listened to the tapes. It was like experiencing the trauma anew. I'd sit there, trying to write, and be swamped by waves of emotion, crying so hard my tears would wet the page and smear the words, crying so hard that, at times, I simply ran out of tears. Other times, I'd literally be gasping for air, because there'd be so much pain. But, when I started delving into what that pain was and how it affected me, there was more power in them that I could ever have imagined. Their impact was so much more than I ever realized because I was actually re-living experiences—how a flashback may have taken place, how I feared others' reactions, and I could now see how it impacted those around me. What was most difficult for me was to re-experience how much it hurt my family.

That's what my doctor meant when he said it gets worse before it gets better. I had to go through the experiences again and again, over and over. As I did, there were times my symptoms became dramatically worse, my flashbacks more frequent, my nightmares more intense. Things long pent up were being unleashed. I was afraid, but I wasn't hiding it away. I had hope.

That's why I am doing this now, why I've written this book, so others won't suffer as long as I did, and those around them won't suffer either. If I had known earlier that, by undergoing therapy, I could have helped my family, that might have changed my thinking, and led me to treatment earlier. Because I was hurting the people I least wanted to hurt. The whole reason I went to therapy, initially, was to help them. That was what clicked for me. When I read that article, saw that I had so many of the symptoms, and then read that people were getting better and that was helping the people who cared for them the most...that got me to pick up the phone and led me through the door.

The doctor also made me realize that I needed to love myself, and give myself credit for something, that what I was doing was important because it would impact me too, that it would make my life better. For years, I had beat myself up for not being a better father and husband. But I couldn't help others until I helped myself.

It also helped immensely that Denise became such a big part of the process. When you are undergoing therapy, so much of it is just you and your doctor. It's private. But my handwriting is terrible, and I'm an awful typist. Writing wasn't just hard emotionally, it was hard, period. It wasn't something I had done much of. So I asked Denise to help. She would take what I had written, type it up and print it out for me. Even though she said I was no award-winning actor, I was still pretty good, and there was so much she didn't know, such as the degree to which my traumas impacted every moment of my life. By putting my words on paper, she was able to share that experience with me, learning things she had never known. Now, because she was reading it first, it was easier to talk about it with her later.

I was worried at first. I worried, not so much about whether she was ready to hear everything, but if I was ready for her to hear everything. I figured there might be some things in there that would bother her, but it was important for her to know I was in pain. Ultimately, it might be better for her to read it, process it, and then talk about it. Reading, I think, gave her a chance to get perspective on what was going on with me before hearing it from my own lips.

After several months, it started to click. It became easier to write—and write in more detail. I began to realize that the embarrassment, fear, and shame I had felt for so long was beginning to fade. Even though it was difficult, even though I was still symptomatic, I looked forward to meeting with the doctors. I looked forward to documenting my experiences in writing. I looked forward to sharing them with Denise. Every waking moment was no longer about concealing things. It was just the opposite. Ever so slowly, I was beginning to feel like I could approach the trauma at McDonald's and not be overwhelmed by it.

The whole time, my doctors were educating me about PTSD, answering every question I had, letting me know that what I was experiencing was not just common to the PTSD experience, but expected. It was reassuring to know that I wasn't crazy, and that many other people had gone through it. It gave me a sense of peace to know that I wasn't just messed up, that what was wrong with me had a name. With each reliving of the trauma, first through talking, then through listening, then through writing, I began to desensitize the experience.

The next step was to read my words aloud, actually speak them out to myself in front of a mirror. That was a whole new experience, another level of re-experiencing and reliving, one that caused a whole new set of emotional reactions. I'd cry again when I thought I couldn't cry any more. I just had to keep going to that well, to keep reaching down and pulling up whatever was left down there. Each time, I'd think, "How can I possibly go through this again? How can it be so hard each time?" But, by then, I knew I'd gone through it before. At a certain point, I realized that, no matter how painful it was, each time I worked through a trauma, I knew I could handle the next one, because I felt so empowered by the way I had worked through the previous one. What I was going through wasn't a sign of weakness, but a sign of strength. *I can do this.*

I was fortunate to have such caring doctors. I was still being treated for pain, and it was vital that the medical and therapeutic sides of my treatment were compatible, to make sure I wouldn't be prescribed something that might cause a negative reaction. When I started, I was hesitant to let my pain doctors know about my PTSD as I was afraid of what they might think.

Cognitive behavioral therapy, the process described above whereby I would talk about the experience, listen to it, write it down, then speak the words aloud, had to take place for each traumatic incident: McDonald's, physical therapy, County Stadium, and Terry's death. At any point, I was always free to return to a trauma, to revisit it or talk about it. I can't say it got easier with each event because it didn't. In many ways, re-experiencing Terry's death, with all the guilt I felt, may have been the toughest of all. I still have a hard time forgiving myself for not being more explicit about how I felt about him. I would give anything to have another five minutes with him.

As I moved through the traumas, my confidence in the process grew, as did my commitment and my belief. Ever so slowly, I noticed various symptoms becoming less pronounced. Not every revving engine caused my heart to race or triggered a flashback. The sense of vigilance and stress I felt from constantly being on guard lessened. I found it easier to relate to Denise and the girls and stopped hiding. I stopped working simply to avoid dealing with my life. When I went for treatment, instead of being afraid of being recognized, I started to hope I might, so I could tell people that I was getting help and encourage others to take the same steps.

Chapter 15

*W*hen I awoke the morning of February 25, 2011, it was still early, the morning light just breaking through the darkness. I looked at my phone to check the time and to see if there were any messages. As I did, it occurred to me that I didn't have a nightmare. Not a single one. For the first time in twenty-nine years, I had slept through the night. I had to think for a moment to make sure I wasn't just too groggy to remember one, but that had never happened before. I had slept seven hours straight without waking. It was a strange sensation. I actually felt rested. For years, I'd wake up feeling about as exhausted as when I'd gone to bed. This was different. I felt energized.

I was also a little scared. The doctors had told me that nothing in this process would be instantaneous and it was important for me to hear this. When Denise was first typing up my notes about PTSD she said, "This just doesn't make sense." She couldn't understand how it could be playing such a dominant role in every aspect of my life.

I told her to think about PTSD as a monster with tentacles. Each tentacle was an aspect of PTSD that had wrapped itself around me. It was like a kraken, the sea monster, that was always grabbing at me, always pulling me down, keeping me from catching my breath, from living.

In therapy, my doctors and I spent a lot of time just separating each tentacle from the other and then, through my repeated re-telling of the events, desensitizing myself not just to each trauma, but to each aspect of each trauma, trying to pull the tentacles loose. I knew we had been making progress—the tentacles weren't such a tangle any more—but now they were letting go. And that tentacle that manifested itself in nightmares had been there so long, and been such a part of me, that I could hardly believe it had let go. I was finally breaking through the surface and emerging back into the world.

I felt like jumping around the room, screaming and yelling like the Sox had just won the World Series again, but I am incredibly superstitious. I hadn't actually won yet, but it was a big hit that drove in a few runs and put me in a position to come back. For the first time ever, I felt like I could come back.

If you're familiar with Red Sox history, you know to never take anything for granted. Every Sox fan remembers the 1986 World Series, when they were one out away from beating the Mets. Mookie Wilson bounced a simple groundball right through Bill Buckner's legs. The lockers were already covered with plastic and buckets of champagne were being wheeled in. That's what "one base at a time" means anyway, right? Don't get ahead of yourself. Just stay patient. I didn't want to jinx myself. Besides, in our family, we had a little superstition not to talk about nightmares before breakfast because, if you do, they might come true. Usually, by the time breakfast was over, you'd forget all about them. I never would. I'd never talked about my nightmares, but I also wasn't about to talk about this. So I kept it to myself. I wanted to make sure I made the play and got the out at first.

The next night, Saturday, I was actually excited about going to sleep. I was still worried, but at least I could tell myself that, even if I had a nightmare, I now knew it was possible for them to end. If nothing else, that gave me a great boost of confidence in my therapy. I knew we were on the right track. I fell asleep like I always did, to the sound of the television in the background. I made sure not to change anything. I went through all my usual routines and drifted off. I didn't wake again until morning. My head wasn't pounding, my sheets weren't soaked with sweat, and I wasn't exhausted. For the second night in a row, I did not have a nightmare. When I slept though the next night, I finally believed it. Twenty-nine years of hell, of spending every day dreading the next night, were over.

I don't know if there is any way for me to adequately explain what that felt like. That kraken was letting go and getting weaker. There were still some tentacles attached, but I was on the surface now, breathing easier, looking to the sky, basking in the sun, knowing I would stay afloat, confident that, over the coming weeks and days, I would become freer and more buoyant. When I told Denise and then my doctor, the next day in therapy, I could not help crying. This time, they were tears of joy, of relief.

I can't overstate the impact that the cessation of my nightmares had on my life. Instead of being exhausted all the time, I felt rested. I no longer felt I had to work myself to exhaustion just so I could sleep. I was no longer afraid of the night. Instead, I welcomed it.

Several years before, in an attempt to sleep better, I'd been tested for sleep apnea. In the test, they monitor your brain waves and breathing while you sleep and try to determine your sleep patterns—how deeply you sleep, how long it takes to fall asleep, how often you wake up, things like that. With me, they had to perform the test twice, because the results didn't make any sense to them: they thought something had gone wrong with the test. But when the same thing happened the next time, they told me, "Your brain doesn't shut down; it is constantly active." That was no surprise to me but, at the time, of course, I didn't tell them why.

Just because I could sleep through the night didn't mean I became a completely changed person. I wasn't. Years of suffering from that particular symptom had affected many aspects of my life. Without even realizing it, I'd adopted behaviors, strategies, and attitudes that allowed me to cope with the nightly presence of nightmares, and those were habits that were hard to break. I still worked too much and, although I was slowly getting better, I still had a great deal of work to do to become more emotionally open and forthright. But I did have the feeling I had rounded one very important base and could see my way to the next. Sleeping without nightmares was validation that all of the difficult months of counseling I'd been through were actually working.

My doctors were wonderful. In addition to the cognitive therapy, they were also teaching me ways to deal with PTSD symptoms on my own, what to do when I felt anxious and fearful, or sensed the onset of a flashback or panic attack. Whenever I felt one coming on, I'd try to make use of breathing and relaxation techniques to control panic and my heartrate and use positive imagery to replace the negative images that would crop up. In regard to Terry, for instance, when I thought of him, I had to learn to replace the images of his death with happier images from our lives together. Believe it or not, you can train your brain to do that.

I was incrementally getting to a place where I was no longer scared of my symptoms or of PTSD. It stopped dominating my life. And I knew that, if I ever began to feel otherwise, if I could not deflect the symptoms on my own, that, anytime of the day or night, my doctors were available to take my call. They let me know that was okay. For so long, I had thought there was no one I could share my feelings with. Now I knew that either Denise or my doctors would listen anytime I needed them. That was incredibly comforting.

I tried to keep each improvement in perspective. My doctors had warned me that progress wouldn't be a straight line—I wasn't just going to break into a home run trot. There were times my progress would slow, perhaps even go into reverse for a while. They prepared me for that so, when it happened, I wouldn't see it as a defeat, as failure on my part, but as something normal, even expected. It was just another step toward where I eventually wanted to be, even if it meant slowing down or taking the occasional step back.

I'm a unique case because, fortunately, I have not had that experience as much as many others PTSD survivors. But still, when it happens, or I sense that it might be happening, I'm not scared of it. It doesn't dominate my life. I know what steps to take next. I'll always be able to talk with someone or get more counseling. It's not like I had PTSD and now I don't. I have PTSD and always will, but now it is in remission. It does not define me or my actions. I wear it as a badge of honor, a scar from a battle I fought for many years and from which I emerged victorious.

The start of the 2011 baseball season was right around the corner. In only a few weeks, we were all back outside working on the field. And, although I loved being at Fenway, there was always one issue I had being there. Ten or twenty times a day I would walk past those seats by the visitor's dugout where my Dad, Mom, Terry, and Chip had sat together before I was born, watching a game together. That had always been a powerful experience for me, but one I had to be careful of as well, because it would make me think about Terry and my Dad and would sometimes trigger strong emotions. I might suddenly be overwhelmed by sadness, causing my feelings to spiral out of control. Now that we were outside again, I realized that, when I walked by those seats, they were still a trigger, but in a very different way. The emotional reaction no longer felt threatening. Instead, seeing those seats gave me a feeling of warmth. I still miss Terry but, when I look at those seats now, I don't think so much about what was lost by his passing, but what we had together as a family, all the wonderful experiences. I think of him coaching me or taking me places, showing me how to cut someone's lawn or making that banner in our basement and then smuggling it into Riverfront Stadium. It's comforting to look over there now. I feel as if my loved ones are there, watching over me.

In the summer, there are tours of Fenway and, on a given day, maybe a thousand or fifteen hundred people walk through the park. I'll often come across the groups and sometimes overhear the conversations of the fans. Everybody has their own special memory of the park, whether it's your first game or something deeply personal that stays with you. That's one of the special things about Fenway and what makes my job so unique. Fenway Park creates memories and, by maintaining the field, I feel that our crew is a part of that legacy. The tour groups usually contain generations of fans moving thorough the park together. I've lost track of how many times I've heard a grandparent say to a small child, "That's where we sat when we came here with your Dad," or seen a father point out to a daughter where he sat with his parents the first time. Perhaps they've passed since then, but it's a memory they share that will live forever and be passed down in a family for generations.

For a long time, I didn't know how that felt. In fact, it sometimes made me uncomfortable to hear those conversations, triggering sad emotions. Someone would meet me for the first time and, because they knew I worked at Fenway, they'd bubble over with excitement, telling me about seeing a game with their brother or special friend, driving in from the suburbs and then coming up the tunnel to see the field for the first time. I was always polite and always listened, but it wasn't a comfortable experience for me. I didn't relate to it in a positive way. But, in the spring of 2011, I did. The memories that came when I walked past those seats were not about loss; now, they were about what I had gained. They were about love. It's amazing how a few empty seats in a ballpark can be so powerful. I love hearing those stories now, and I enjoy telling my own story.

I had never had a hard time talking about how proud I was to be Terry's brother, about all of his accomplishments and all the things he did for me, but I was always selective. I never went too deep into his role as a father figure, because doing that could trigger an unwanted flashback—I'd start to run out of breath or well up with tears. Although it is still emotional, it no longer bothers me. I love talking about Terry. When I give talks, I like talking about that aspect of our relationship the most. I encourage people to reach out to their loved ones and let them know how they feel, not to miss out on that opportunity like I did. I'm always amazed by how many people approach me afterward and thank me for doing that, who find the fact that I can talk about Terry now so moving, because so many people have had similar experiences with a loved one they have lost. If talking about Terry brings me to tears now, I'm not embarrassed at all. I can hardly believe that. For too long, I worried too much about how others would judge me, that, by expressing my emotions, I might be viewed as weak. They don't. People see it as I do now: a sign of strength. Truly, it takes more courage to express your feelings than it does to keep them hidden.

A few years before I began treatment, and long before I realized I had PTSD, Denise and Cacky told me I should write a book about all my medical issues and the physical adversity I had faced. They asked if reading such a book would have helped me when I was younger. I believed it would have. They said, "Write your life story. If it helps one person, it will be worth doing."

I wasn't sold. I couldn't imagine anyone wanting to read a book about me and didn't want people to think I was just seeking attention, but Denise was pretty convincing. She said it wasn't about me; it was about helping others.

Denise and Cacky were extremely perceptive. When I give motivational talks, people often say I should write a book about overcoming adversity. They figured out that writing a book might be a way for me to realize how I was behaving and begin to take positive steps toward correcting these behaviors. In many ways, they anticipated the therapy that would be so beneficial to me. They knew that, if I was completely honest about what had happened in my life, the process of documenting it would prove to be cathartic. Cacky had learned this studying art therapy. They didn't relate it to PTSD but to my pain, my struggles with pain, and overcoming adversity and not giving in. Yes, they thought I could help someone else, but they also thought that writing a book would help me. It was a way to start the process. They were tired of walking on eggshells around me, not knowing what to say or how to say it. When Denise said that, if the book only helped one person, it would be worth it, that one person she was talking about was me.

I tried to write that book, at least I started to, focusing on the positive, the benefits of working hard and fighting through your challenges, no matter what. But, even then, I knew I was only telling half the story. I knew I had no intention of ever revealing what was going on inside me, so that project was doomed from the start. Without telling the whole story, I just couldn't exorcise all the drama and trauma. I think I was afraid that, if I wrote too much, somebody was going to notice that I was really messed up inside. I wrote a proposal and started writing, but I was unable to open up and tell the full story.

Now, after undergoing treatment, everything is different. As I continued with my treatment and moved forward, learning to control what remained of my symptoms, I was reminded of the impact that one small article had on my life. Had I never read it—or if it had never been written—I might never have received treatment. I may never have helped set up the Run for Home Base at Fenway Park each year and never realized that I suffered from the same issue.

I don't want another person to go through what I did. As I got better, I began to feel a responsibility to those suffering PTSD. I was blessed to be in a position that provided some public recognition and put me in contact with the media. The more time that passed, the more comfortable I became with the idea of making my story public. If I told the whole truth of my story, maybe I could help someone and spread the word that PTSD wasn't just something that afflicted members of the military. Had I just known that, I might have made the connection to my own symptoms, years earlier. Knowledge has power. It can change lives.

All through my treatment, I told no one but my family but, as the regular season approached, I decided it was time to let others know I had PTSD. Just a few days before Opening Day, I called a couple of my colleagues from the grounds crew into my office. I had no idea how anyone would react. As straightforwardly as possible, I told them I had PTSD and that I had been receiving treatment during the off season. I also apologized because I knew that, at times, I had allowed PTSD to affect my behavior. I couldn't have been more surprised by their reactions. They didn't look at me strangely or judge me and, most importantly, afterwards, they didn't treat me any differently than they had before. I was still Dave.

Over the next day or two, I spoke to everyone else I felt I needed to speak to with the Red Sox, from my boss to Larry Lucchino, then the team president. I apologized if I had allowed it to affect my behavior in the past. Not one person reacted with anything but understanding and compassion. I never felt a second of awkwardness. And, when I told my close friends and other family members, I got similar reactions. Not one person said anything rude or made an inappropriate facial expression or anything. In fact, some people even began to share their own stories about their own similar experiences or that of their family members or friends. PTSD can afflict anyone, from any walk of life. It doesn't recognize gender, race, or religion. Any human being who has undergone trauma can suffer from PTSD.

All those worries I had for so many years about being seen as weak proved groundless. No one changed the way they acted around me. No one walked on eggshells. The guys on the crew who knew kept busting my chops the way they always had.

Still, it remained, very much, a private matter. Although I had no problem telling people in the waiting room at my doctor's office that I was being seen for PTSD, no one from the press knew about it—but there wasn't anything strange about that. People don't buy the paper in the morning, turn on their computer or the television to hear about the groundskeeper. A short time later, during the Yankees first visit to Fenway that year, I was standing by the field waiting for batting practice to end when Buster Olney from ESPN stepped up to me and introduced himself. Of course, I knew who Buster was from seeing him around the ballpark, but we had never spoken before.

"David, you've been doing this a long time. How'd you ever get started?" he asked.

"My dream was always to make it to the majors," I told him. "My grandfather played in the majors in 1902 and I wanted to follow in his footsteps. That's all I wanted to do while I was growing up. But, after high school, I was hit by a car and my leg was crushed. I thought my dreams were crushed, but my family encouraged me not to see what happened as a roadblock, but a challenge, to find a passion and pursue my dreams. Eventually, I studied horticulture and worked real hard, and that was how I ended up becoming a groundskeeper."

It wasn't a long conversation, just a few minutes. Then batting practice ended and I had to get back to work. I told him it was nice to meet him but now I had work to do. I nearly forgot all about it.

Several weeks later, I was at work and Denise noticed that I had received an email from Buster. She called to tell me she thought I should read it right away. In the email, he explained that he had told my story to some people at ESPN, and that they wanted to tell my story as a feature on their newsmagazine "E-60." He knew nothing about my PTSD. I was flattered, but a little embarrassed. I didn't want people to think I was trying to get attention. But Denise talked me into it. She said that, if I told my story about overcoming adversity, it would give other people hope. I called Buster back and agreed to cooperate.

They started coming to Fenway periodically to film for the story and, over time, I started to trust both Buster and his producer, Heather Lombardo. I started opening up and, over the next year and a half, I told him everything—about how I had PTSD, about my treatment, about the way I had a drinking problem and had quit, everything. The segment was supposed to run at the end of the 2012 season, but the Red Sox weren't playing well, so they decided to hold it until the following spring when there would be more interest. On Patriot's Day in 2013, the Boston Marathon bombings took place. Just after that, Heather called and asked if they could talk some more, because they thought that, in the wake of the bombing, the story might be even more helpful, because so many had been traumatized by the experience.

The eleven-minute segment, titled "Fenway's Keeper," aired on May 2, 2013, and was posted online with a print story written by veteran reporter Steve Marantz. The day after the story appeared, I walked out onto the field and a ballplayer on the opposing team stopped me. He said he and his teammates had seen the story and talked about it, and that they all agreed that now they felt they could go to their own team psychologist if they ever felt they needed to. He thanked me for speaking up.

That was when I first began to realize how much impact this story might have. I was soon stunned both by the number of people it had reached and their responses. I received hundreds of letters from all over the country from people telling me they had decided to stop drinking, had made an appointment with a psychologist, or had talked to a family member about PTSD. Until then, I never realized how much my story could touch people, or how useful it was for people to hear a story like mine. Like me, many people had thought PTSD only affected members of the military and veterans.

I was occasionally recognized before but, after the feature appeared, I was recognized much more often, not just at the ballpark, but when I was out at the hardware store or the grocery store or a restaurant. Many ask about PTSD, mention that they know someone with PTSD, or someone that they think might be suffering from PTSD. Not so long ago, I would have been embarrassed by that, but now I'm proud and happy to talk about it and eager to tell people that help is available and point them that direction. PTSD is treatable. I realize now, as a survivor, that is my responsibility, my way of saying thanks for the help I have received. I would feel terrible if somebody asked me about my PTSD and I didn't tell them the truth.

I'm even approached by people from the military. Even though it's well known that many combat vets have PTSD, that doesn't mean that every victim asks for treatment. Even military vets can still feel a stigma about having PTSD. Just as I did, many veterans try to "soldier on" and suffer alone.

Even though the military and the VA work hard to get returning soldiers and vets into treatment, each PTSD victim is unique. An approach that might get one person into treatment may not work with another. For me, it was one small magazine article. After one talk I gave before a military squadron, several members came up to me later to tell me they were going to look into treatment. Sometime later, the squadron leader told me that, in the week after the talk, the base psychologist told him that more than a half dozen members who had attended my presentation went to see him. Each man or woman who admits to suffering from PTSD can lead others to treatment. If we can just keep that chain going, all those small steps taken together become very powerful. Each person who steps from the shadows leads others to do the same.

Since the E-60 story, I've been approached by hundreds of people about PTSD. I told Buster Olney and Heather Lombardo that they've helped us touch lives in ways I never fathomed, the same way I hope to touch lives with this book. That's why I feel it's important to let people know that my story didn't end with some kind of miracle cure, where I was suddenly free of PTSD. It doesn't work that way. It's an ongoing process.

Before the story aired, over the course of the 2011 season, my symptoms continued to retreat, my ability to control them increased, and eventually I stopped seeing a therapist on a regular basis. That didn't mean my treatment stopped. I'm far more aware now of those times where I might be vulnerable, when I might need extra help. I'm still sensitive to the anniversaries of my accidents and the deaths of my father and Terry. Although I have strategies I can employ when I feel symptoms beginning to return, my doctors are always on call. When I feel I need them, I can always get an appointment to talk. I take a proactive approach, before anything gets out of hand.

Sooner or later, an old trigger is going to flare up, or a new trauma may happen. In the past, I just would have suffered in silence and carried that burden internally. Now, whether it's a new trauma or an old trigger, I've learned that, the sooner I go talk to the doctor, the better. I've learned that it does no good at all to try to keep everything inside, to think that, somehow, I can handle this by myself. I can't. There are many people available to help. I am no longer ashamed to ask for help when I need it.

Tragedies and the deaths of those I know and love are particularly difficult for me. Later in 2011, my dear friend, Gary, my boss at the Brewers, called to let me know he had cancer. The news really shook me up. Gary and I had worked side by side all those years in Milwaukee. Though he was my boss, he treated me as an equal, as a brother and a friend. No matter how many times my health issues took me away from work or made it hard for me to do my job, he was always there, helping me get to work when I couldn't drive, asking me if there was anything he could do. He is one of many people who made me the person I am today.

His prognosis was not good and, as soon as he told me the sad news, I arranged to see my doctor the next day to talk about it. I went back several more times until I could put his illness in perspective and integrate that into my life. I did so without embarrassment. Even in the waiting room, if someone says, "Hey, aren't you groundskeeper for the Red Sox?" today, I say, "Yes, I sure am." And, if they ask, "What are you doing here?" I answer, "I'm going to see my psychologist. I have PTSD." That's doesn't make me special; it's just part of who I am.

Gary passed away on October 11 of that year, and, although I still found his passing difficult—I still can't attend funerals—because I had gone for help in advance, his passing did not become another trigger for PTSD. Instead, it became another sign of the strength I have gained through coming to terms with my disorder. Gary, in his own way, showed me just how strong I was becoming. He left me an everlasting gift, one that I can now help pass on to others.

Let me tell you just one of many such stories. My buddy, Bob, operates a TV camera during some games. He has always been exceptionally helpful and the respect he shows my crew and me is remarkable. Bob knows I am a PTSD survivor, something we've talked about many times. On several different occasions, I've tried to take him to lunch or find another way to thank him, but he always politely declines, saying he just treats people like he wants to be treated. One day, I realized I had an extra Red Sox grounds crew coat from a couple seasons past. It was old but unused. I put it in a bag and asked a crewmember to take it to him. I warned the crewmember that Bob would refuse to take it, but to insist, and to be sure to leave the bag with him. Sure enough, Bob didn't want to accept it at first but finally did. He later put it in his luggage to fly home.

A few months later, when Bob returned to Fenway, he shared a special story with me. Bob lives in Florida and is an avid fisherman, often going out surfcasting with a group of four other guys he has known for years. Shortly after returning to Florida with the jacket, one of his fishing buddies called and said he knew a doctor who specializes in treating military veterans who have PTSD. The doctor said he was wondering if he could bring a patient he was treating to go fishing. "Before you say okay," he said, "I need to fill you in on a little bit of this gentleman's background." His patient, who we'll call Joe, had gone on a number of top-secret missions, and one of his symptoms was a violent temper. When he was hospitalized, there were times he'd had to be restrained and was even locked in a padded room. When he left the hospital, he only did so under armed guard.

The doctor also said he had not spoken in years. He was hoping, if Joe could get out and have a positive fishing experience, it could be helpful. In part, because Bob knew about my PTSD experience, he wasn't worried about being with Joe, and understood that the outing might be helpful. Bob said he would be happy to have Joe join them.

Several days later, the guys were down at the beach getting ready to fish when a van pulled up, a couple of armed guards got out, and the doctor and Joe followed them. Everyone introduced themselves. Joe just nodded. They set him up with a rod and everyone started fishing. Everyone but Joe was having pretty good luck, and Bob was keeping tabs on him, trying to make sure he had a good time. Just then, he looked out to sea and saw a large, dark shadow. Bob pointed it out to Joe and suggested he cast that direction. Joe did as Bob suggested, and "WHAM!" something really big hit the bait and took off. The battle was on. For the next ninety minutes, as the rest of the fishermen cheered him on and gave advice, Joe fought with the fish on the end of his line. At last, the exhausted fish gave up and Joe was able to land it in the shallows. No one could believe their eyes. The fish was a blacktip shark, thirteen-feet long, weighing hundreds of pounds. They celebrated like they had won the World Series and took pictures of Joe and his amazing catch.

Bob asked Joe if he wanted to see how they take the hook out of the shark's mouth, so they could release the shark. Joe nodded yes. When they got down beside the shark's head, Bob asked Joe if he wanted to take the hook out himself. Joe nodded and carefully took the hook out while looking deeply into the eye of the shark. He then watched the shark, exhausted but unhurt, slowly swim away. Everyone could tell that Joe found the experience moving. Afterwards, he went over and sat down on the edge of the breakwater. He got up and paced back and forth, before sitting down again. He then got up and walked over to Bob and in a broken voice spoke the first words anyone heard him utter in twenty years.

"Are you part of the hospital?" he asked.

"No, Joe." the doctor said. "These are a group of fishing buddies who fish here regularly. Bob actually works in television and travels around filming MLB baseball games."

Joe turned and took a few steps, looking around, then paused for a long moment and walked back over to Bob and, in a shaky voice, asked, "Have you been to Fenway Park?"

"Yes," Bob said. "It is one of my favorite places to go. My buddy is the groundskeeper."

"The Red Sox are my favorite team," Joe said quietly as he smiled.

The group soon started putting away their fishing gear and, as Bob packed up to leave, he remembered that he still had the grounds crew jacket in the trunk of his car. He got the bag and gave it to Joe.

"Here's a little something for you," Bob said. "I hope you enjoy it."

He said his goodbyes, went to his car, and drove away before Joe opened the bag.

A few weeks later, Bob's phone rang with an unfamiliar number listed. Bob was surprised because his number was private. It was the doctor. Bob asked how he got his number and the doctor explained that, because of Joe's high rank, security staff had recorded Bob's license plate number and were able to track him down. The doctor told Bob that, after Joe opened the bag Bob gave him, he took out the coat and promptly put it on. He liked the coat so much he kept wearing it. Over the following two days, Joe suddenly started inter-acting for the first time with fellow patients also suffering from symptoms of PTSD. He encouraged them to not give up and keep working to feel better. He said, if he could start feeling better, that he hoped they could start feeling better too. The other patients, knowing the depth of his troubles, were stunned and inspired. A few days later, he asked his doctor if he could telephone his family. He wanted to talk with them and let them know he was feeling better and getting treatment. Joe spoke to his family for the first time in a very long time. One of the things he told his wife and son were, "When I get out of here I want to take us all to see a Red Sox game at Fenway Park." In the next weeks, Joe made rapid progress. Soon, he began the transition to return to his home and rebuild the relationship with his wife and son.

The day Bob told me the story, he also said that Joe and his family were supposed to be at Fenway the following day, the hundredth anniversary celebration of Fenway Park. I wanted to meet him and give them a special tour, but Bob didn't know how to contact them. Over the next few months, I often thought of Joe, and I hoped he and his family made it to Fenway Park.

Later that year, Bob and his friends were fishing again when a stranger approached and asked, "Are you Bob?" He explained that he was Joe's son and just wanted to thank Bob for his kindness and tell him how wonderful it was to have his Dad back in his life.

Even after twenty years, just like me, Joe had found the courage to get treatment and move, one base at a time, toward recovery. And, just like me, he had found his way to Fenway Park.

Chapter 16

I had always loved dogs. Following my dad's death, when I was three, my mom brought home a Pug named Duke. She thought Duke would be therapeutic for me and my brothers. A dog's love and devotion can provide a welcome distraction during difficult times. Duke did that and, over time, became a member of our family. Each of us loved him, especially Terry, who said many times: "After I die, I'm gonna come back as your dog." He truly loved dogs and had a remarkable bond with his Samoyed, Mac, before he passed away. I guess, as a kid, I always thought that he hoped to return as a dog in his next life.

Duke lived until I was sixteen. After he passed, we got a blonde English Cocker Spaniel, who my mom named Alex. I was stuck at home a lot after the accident at McDonald's, so I spent a lot of time with Alex, teaching him basic obedience and tricks. I trained him to recognize his different toys not only by name but when I spelled them out and showed them to him. He even learned to recognize them spelled backwards. I could line up twenty-five toys in a row and he would pick out the one I named or spelled. I nicknamed him

"Alex the Wonder Dog" and even tried to get on *Late Night with David Letterman* for one of his "Stupid Pet Tricks" segments.

Denise and I had two pugs when the girls were younger, but it had been a while since I'd had a dog in my life. In 2014, Denise told me that getting a service dog might be good for me, as it might ground me, give me confidence, and help me move safely when in crowded situations. We went online and started researching. I had heard of service dogs but had never really thought of how one could help me. I was familiar with guide dogs for the visually challenged, but soon discovered that service dogs can be beneficial to people struggling with a wide array of disabilities. I was especially surprised to learn just how much of an impact a service dog can have on someone suffering from PTSD. PTSD service dogs can be trained to sense when you're feeling stressed and help calm you. And, for someone like me with mobility issues, help with balance. Dogs are very intuitive and can even be trained to detect when you're experiencing a situation that might serve as a trigger or be dangerous. Studies have shown that the presence of a dog can even help raise levels of serotonin, a "feel-good" hormone and lower blood pressure.

Once I realized the amazing range of what they can do, I became excited about the idea. Although the most intensive part of my PTSD therapy had passed, I began to understand that having a service dog was an extension of my treatment. It would be part of the ongoing process of healing and learning to survive with PTSD. Before undergoing counseling and therapy, I don't think I ever would have believed how much a service dog could impact my life. In fact, I think it would have made me more self-conscious, that the dog would draw unwanted attention and make others even more aware of my scars and my limp. But the more I learned, the more excited I became.

Denise's family had three German shepherds on their farm in Ohio when she was growing up. One dog, Prince, even helped herd the cows and pigs. She had always been impressed by their loyalty and intelligence. Given my issues walking, I needed a large dog that could provide physical support if I were ever knocked off balance and needed to brace myself. We found a private trainer and discussed which would be the right breed for me, and he agreed with our preference for shepherds. During our research phase, a friend tipped us off to the incredible lineage and breeding standards in Eastern Europe, so we were comfortable that their dogs would be far less likely to suffer from hip dysplasia, which is a genetic disorder common among this breed. Ultimately, we found a breeder in Slovakia who had a young, sable-colored German shepherd. I named him Drago, which is Slovakian for "precious."

Before you can meet your dog, the trainer works with him on his basic training and skills, teaching the dog a wide variety of commands and behaviors. While some are simple obedience commands, other training is for specific tasks according to the handler's needs. Every baseball player knows how to throw a baseball, but outfielders throw differently than infielders, as do catchers and pitchers. That's kind of the way it works with service dogs. Drago had to be well trained first, specifically for the things I needed most.

Drago came to live with us on May 9, 2014. I was apprehensive before we met because I didn't want to let him down by not being a great communicator and handler. I'd never had a dog his size before. As soon I looked into his eyes, I felt a wave of emotion. I loved his smile! Any anxiety I had felt immediately melted away as his eyes locked on mine. I could tell I had his full focus and that all he cared about was pleasing me. I wanted to make this work more than ever.

The following day, we took Drago to the vet for his first check-up. The vet scanned his chip and told us his birthday was Sept 23. Chills ran through me as the hair stood up on my arms. Denise and I looked at each other and said, "That's Terry's birthday." I immediately thought of my brother and what he had said all those years ago. I looked at Drago and he looked right into my eyes. It felt like he was looking into my soul. It is a moment I'll always remember. His golden hazel eyes were reassuring to me.

Still, we had a lot of work to do together creating a trusting bond. It was a lot of work for both of us as we learned the commands to ensure that I was communicating properly with him and that he understood my needs. Even though the trainer is still part of our lives and will occasionally help train Drago for a new task, I had to learn to become a dog handler, to become consistent with my commands and give him as much guidance and support as he gives me. Among other things, Drago had to learn to sense my anxiety and, when he did, to help me cope.

Just as important was the training we, as a family, had to undertake. We had to learn how to interact with Drago and give him the proper commands in the proper ways, so he would not become confused. It was important for both Denise and our daughter to learn how to do that, in the event they had to stay with Drago when I wasn't present. In one example, although Drago had received some training for mobility assistance, because of the twenty surgeries I have had on my right knee, he had to learn to work on my left side. He also had to learn to go up and down stairs the way I do, one step at a time so I don't put too much stress on my surgical right knee. And I had to learn to remain aware of him being beside me. He learned different commands depending on how close I need him beside me, ranging from three feet to touching me. As we became more familiar with each other, he became an extension of me, as if he were almost another part of my body. Drago's calm confidence built confidence in me and us as a team. He has improved my quality of life as well as my family's.

One day, shortly after Drago came into my life, he proved just how valuable he could be. I stumbled and fell at home. Fortunately, the fall wasn't serious, but I couldn't easily get to my feet by myself. Denise was in another part of the house and couldn't hear me calling out to her. In the past, this would have been stressful. Drago rushed to my side. I was able to use him for support to get back on my feet. I gave him the bark command to get Denise's attention, then told him to alert Denise and bring her to me. She heard Drago bark and, in a few moments, he found her and led her to my side.

Each day that we worked together strengthened our relationship. Today, I am amazed at how responsive he is. All I have to do is whisper a command and he instantly obeys. Now he's able to sense my needs before I even tell him what to do.

I consider Drago the most amazing medical tool I have ever experienced, empowering me with the confidence to live with both my mental and physical challenges. The more familiar we become with one another, the more confident I feel. From the start, I was far less self-conscious about my limp and less afraid of any possible triggers or flashbacks. Far from being embarrassed by having Drago at my side, I am proud of the way he helps me, just as I am proud to be a PTSD survivor. And just as I want to bring awareness about PTSD to others, so they don't suffer, I also want to spread the word about how much help a service dog can be and what a life-changing experience having a dog like Drago is.

I had to inform the Red Sox about Drago and the role he would now play in my life. The Sox already knew about my physical challenges and PTSD and had always been supportive but, before I brought Drago to Fenway Park, I contacted my bosses and the vice president of Human Resources. I let them know he was in my life and would be with me at work at the ballpark and told them how much I would appreciate their support. I sensed that there was some hesitation about having Drago with me on the field, and I assured them that he wouldn't be there unless I was certain that his behavior could be controlled. Out of respect to the field, the history and aura of Fenway Park, the organization, the players, and the fans, the last thing I wanted was for someone to think that Drago was disrespecting the field. After all, I am often on the field while the players are taking batting practice and working out. We couldn't have a dog chasing after baseballs or squatting on the field to go to the bathroom during practice!

I reassured them that Drago's trainer and I had taken precautions. Drago only barks on command or when he is playing on a break. Otherwise, he is silent. He is trained not to chase balls or respond to other distractions unless I give him permission. He is also trained to not go to the bathroom on grass and go to the bathroom only on command outside the park. He lets me know when he has to go, and I take him outside. Until then, no matter how bad he has to go, he won't until I tell him it is okay to do so.

Drago demonstrated his value during one of his first visits to Fenway. I took him with me to my boss's office. We were discussing how some people can get very intense and raise their voices. After my boss shared his story, I shared mine and imitated a person yelling and swearing. Drago immediately reacted to the stress in my voice, got up from where he was laying by my feet, put his front paws on my lap and pushed his head into my chest to comfort me. My boss was startled. "Wow," he said, "What is he doing?" I explained that Drago was trained to react that way when he detected that I was feeling stress and that, by placing his paws on me and pressing onto my chest, he was interrupting the situation by providing deep compression therapy, forcing me to focus on him and not on what was upsetting me. My boss was amazed. I hadn't said anything to Drago; he just sensed that he might be needed.

Not long after, I was alone in my office with Drago when I began experiencing a flashback. He snapped into action without a word from me, pressing himself against me until I assured him that I was fine.

I took my time introducing Drago to the field to make certain he knew how to behave properly. At first, I only took him onto the field in the morning on non-game days, when there was little activity in the park, long before it came alive with tour groups and other events. I put him on a leash and slowly led him around the park. I allowed him to explore all the nooks and crannies, sniffing around the dugout, the base of the Green Monster, and the bullpens so he could become familiar with the new place. I wanted him to become accustomed to the feel of the warning track beneath his feet, and all the smells—the lingering scent of hot dogs, popcorn, and everything else. This was going to be an important place in both our lives. He needed to feel comfortable and confident in that environment and to maintain his composure and focus.

I worked with him to lay down on command, like we did at home, except now he was on Fenway's hallowed turf, while I was working on the field with the grounds crew cutting the grass, watering down the infield clay, or doing other maintenance. I gradually introduced him to the sounds of lawn mowers and water squirting from hoses. Then I eased him into my pre-game responsibilities on game days.

His response was outstanding, staying under command like that and following his training. Over time, I began to bring him out on the field when there was even more activity, taking him onto the field on game days as the players were working out and taking batting practice. He grew accustomed to the sound of the crack of the bat, to players calling out and joking with each other, and to seeing baseballs bouncing across the infield and rocketing off the wall. Soon, I had him out on the field as the stands were filling with fans and music and announcements played over the public address system.

I owed it to him to do everything I could to help make this a smooth transition. He did great, laying down patiently on leash, his eyes trained on me, accompanying me onto the field only when I called to him that he was needed or led him out on leash, ignoring fans that would try to call out to him and get his attention or anything else that might be a distraction. All of this helped build our working relationship, an important part of our bond. He trusts me, and I trust him.

The players, of course, were curious and, soon after I began bringing him onto the field, they were asking me about Drago. I explained to them the role he played in my life and they were incredibly understanding. Over time, he has built a great friendship with many of them.

Today, Drago is with me 24/7, sleeping near me all night, and waking up with me in the morning. Our morning routine helps me focus and gives me confidence to face the day.

"Hey, brother. How are you?" I ask, putting my forehead on his and rubbing him behind the ears. My conversations with Drago ground me. In the mornings, I make time to meditate with him, connecting with my breathing and thinking about the day ahead. He goes outside to do his business, then comes in and eats as I'm getting ready. Then we're ready for our day.

Drago and I have an incredible bond. I speak out loud to him and tell him what we're going to do each day, whether it's going to work, having an adventure, taking a break to play, or just going shopping. A true friend, he knows my innermost thoughts, and I swear there are times we communicate telepathically. He loves to ride in the car and is always ready to go. He also loves to fly. We pre-board and, when we get up to leave after the flight, other passengers sitting close to us often say, "Wow! I didn't know he was even there." I know I can always count on him.

Of course, when Drago encounters other people, not everyone understands that he is not a pet. Many assume they can automatically talk to or pet him or allow kids to run up to him. He's working and, in some situations, concentrating pretty intensely on the task at hand, whatever it may be. If he loses focus, it could cost us both dearly.

Most people are thoughtful and respectful when meeting us, however. Drago usually wears a service vest, which makes it clear that he's not just another dog. Still, occasionally, people don't understand that, and will want to approach him and give him a friendly pet. It's best not to approach a service dog unless the handler gives permission. As long as I give Drago his release command, it is okay.

I'm proud to explain to people what a service dog is and the role Drago plays in my life, because each relationship between a service dog and their handler is different. Part of training a service dog is to socialize the dog in many settings, including crowds. From the start, since I planned to bring him to Fenway, I worked with Drago to help build his confidence around large groups of people. Depending on what we are doing, I will sometimes give Drago his release command, so he knows that he is free to engage with fans or that he is allowed to play with his favorite toy.

A service dog can be any size or breed and can be trained by their owner, with support of a trainer or obtained through a training/ service dog organization. But they are not therapy dogs, emotional support dogs, comfort dogs, or pets. A service dog is a working dog. They are considered medical equipment, trained in specific tasks to help a person mitigate their disabilities.

Drago never forgets his role. I learned just how committed he is one day on the field. After batting practice is over there, is time reserved for the grounds crew to prepare the field for the game. I often give Drago his command to lie down on the infield grass, so he can still see me while I'm working. One day before I watered the infield skin on the evening of a special pregame ceremony, I settled Drago. As I started watering the infield clay, other staff started setting up folding chairs for special guests behind the pitcher's mound. Drago is trained to stay in position and not move unless he receives the proper release command. As they continued setting up the chairs, Drago laid there perfectly still keeping an eye on me, right in a spot where one of the chairs had to go. Staff asked him to move but he wouldn't break. They kept going and carefully placed a chair over top of him. He just lay there, perfectly still, with a folding chair over his back! I was facing the other direction and didn't see what was happening. As the guests arrived and began taking their seats, Drago still wouldn't break command. One of the guests understandably didn't want to sit on a chair with a big dog underneath it. Fortunately, Denise was there and saw what was going on. She got permission from security, walked over to Drago, gave him his release command and took him off the field.

I quickly began to realize that Drago not only plays an important role in my life, but that he is also a valuable partner in helping me raise awareness for both PTSD and the role of service dogs. Jennifer Chafitz, a producer for ESPN, noticed pictures of Drago at the ballpark on my Instagram feed (@davidrm3llor) and told me she wanted to do a video feature on our relationship. Once upon a time, I might have felt too self-conscious to say "yes," but now I realize that, to tell my story completely, I have to include Drago. The Red Sox gave permission, and Jennifer and a crew spent several days with us at Fenway Park. Denise and I were interviewed. We explained the role of Drago in my treatment, and the crew shot all sorts of footage of the two of us at Fenway. They showed Drago interacting with some of the players and even put a GoPro on his head, so fans could see the field from his perspective!

The segment, "Dave and Drago," aired on *Sports Center* at the end of the season in 124 countries. The response was phenomenal! As I write this, between Facebook, YouTube, and other platforms, it has been viewed more than 4.2 million times (impressions) and allowed me to reach millions of people with my message about PTSD and the value of service dogs.

Drago has been essential in keeping me grounded and guiding me through these past few years and these difficult experiences. It will be a dark day when time takes him away from me. We're already preparing for that, and have already started training another dog, bred from Drago, his name is Keeper for that inevitability. In fact, a couple of Red Sox players, Ian Kinsler and Rick Porcello, both adopted puppies from that same litter.

I really can't express in words how much Drago has meant to me. Although I've never had a tattoo, I have decided to get one to celebrate his place in my life. In fact, a company named Everence has already encapsulated his DNA in the ink that I will use, making it possible for Drago to be part of me for the rest of my life.

The tattoo will be his paw print placed directly over my heart.

Chapter 17

*O*ver the next few years, my recovery progressed, but I continued to have physical issues. In the spring of 2013, I broke my hip and later slipped on my crutches and injured a tendon on my groin, which sent me to the hospital. In June, I had to have my hip replaced. Physical pain, particularly in my lower back, remained an issue, but my inner pain, my emotional pain, my PTSD, remained in remission.

Then came November 9, 2015. One thousand seven hundred and nineteen days since my last nightmare—four years, eight months, and sixteen days later—I woke in the middle of the night, screaming, and saw Denise looking right at me. Drago woke me by pushing his paws on my chest. Then he stayed right beside me. I knew that, one day, I would have a nightmare again. Everybody has nightmares occasionally and, even though I had gone through PTSD therapy, I was no different. In a way, having a nightmare is a natural thing. After waking, I turned toward all that I had learned during my treatment. I didn't freak out, Drago helped me relax, and I system-atically went through some relaxation techniques and biofeedback to control my heart rate and breathing. The nightmare hadn't been like the others—I hadn't seen or heard a car or smelled French fries or experienced any aspects from my previous traumas. I tried to tell myself it was just a dream. I even managed to fall back asleep and slept without incident the rest of the night.

When I woke in the morning, I wasn't anxious. I wasn't covered with sweat and I didn't feel exhausted. I had had a nightmare but, as far as I could determine, it was just that. I knew that, sooner or later, this would happen and, in a funny way, I was sort of proud of it. I had used what I had learned and taken control of the event. I had prepared myself. Nightmares no longer had the power over me they once had.

There was no indication that it had been caused by an old trigger or there was some new trigger to worry about. I went about my day as usual but wasn't unduly worried about going to sleep. The nightmare had not dominated my day. I didn't dread going to sleep that night and went to bed just as I had the previous 1,720 days.

I awoke with a start. The dream was more detailed this time. I was back home in Piqua, in the house I grew up in, where I'd played Wiffle ball in the backyard, learned to cut grass, and had so many other wonderful experiences. Drago was with me. We heard a commotion outside and went to the back door. Coming from the neighbor's backyard into ours were two pickup trucks, engines racing and roaring, filled with men, all of them angry, screaming and yelling. When they saw us, the truck veered toward me. Drago left my side and jumped in front of me, to save me from being run down.

I woke screaming with Drago on me.

This was far more disturbing. Vehicles were involved, and they had been trying to run me down. It was much more detailed, much more frightening. I recognized immediately that this dream might be more than just a nightmare. Fortunately, both Denise and Drago were beside me. Once upon a time, I would have tried to ignore it, bury it away, let it fester, and think of it as some kind of weakness. Now I was a survivor. I knew what to do.

First thing the next morning, I called my doctor. I was going to be proactive. I'd done that before, when I learned that Gary had cancer and even after the Boston marathon bombings, not because I needed help but before I needed help, when I worried that an emotionally disturbing event might turn into something larger and uncontrollable. That's such an important thing for PTSD victims and their families to know, that there might be setbacks, and that there is nothing wrong with asking for help before you are in crisis.

I saw my doctor several times over the next few weeks, and we talked a lot about how this was normal, that it didn't mean all the tentacles were coming back and pulling me down, or that all the progress I had made was gone. I didn't have to start all over again. This was just a small stumble in a much larger journey. I now had the means to ask for help, to get back up, and continue moving forward.

Knock on wood, I haven't had a nightmare since. I don't think of myself as anything special. I'll likely have another nightmare, another trauma. I'm more confident than ever I'll know exactly what to do. I'll ask for help.

In February of 2016, I had another spinal cord stimulator put in. They had been of some help before but my left lower back was really bothering me, and we decided to try it again. My left buttock was in an almost constant state of cramping and sometimes the pain went all the way down to my foot. I met with my surgeon from Beth Israel Deaconess Medical Center, who is very accomplished at stimulator surgery. We met just before the operation and discussed how we hoped the procedure would help with my lower back. Then he asked, "Is there any other pain you'd like to address?" He explained that, if there was, during the operation he could try get the stimulator to take care of that as well.

"I've had twenty surgeries on my right knee," I said. "I've had knee replacement surgery, but I've had knee pain in my leg since I was hit by a car on July 10, 1981. If you can reduce my pain even a little, that would be a bonus."

"Let me see if I can do something while I'm in there."

The stimulator he was implanting had a greater capacity and was more technologically advanced than the first stimulators I had tried. They had only three or four electrodes, whereas this newer version, made by a different company, had sixteen electrodes, all attached to a paddle that would be put in place on my spinal cord, adjusted during surgery, sutured to the vertebrae ligament and eventually held in place by scar tissue. This gave the surgeon more opportunities to send pain-blocking impulses into the nervous system. I can change voltage by way of a remote control.

In my earlier surgeries, the doctor would sometimes wake me during surgery to test the implants, which I found painful and disturbing. This time, he was able to test the implants by computer, to determine where the signal was going and what nerves it was blocking without waking me. Normally, the device isn't turned on and tested until the patient's first follow-up appointment but, in my case, since I'd had stimulators implanted before, I was in the recovery room right after surgery when the doctor and the Medtronics manufacturer's representative and technician stopped by to see how I was doing.

"Why don't we try this now?" the doctor said.

"Go for it," I said.

The Medtronic rep turned it on and, instantly, the hairs stood up on my arms and on the back of my neck, but not due to any electric impulse. It was because the results were so profound and so immediate. Not only was the pain gone in my left lower back, but I smiled and started to cry at the same time.

"This is the first time, since 1981, I literally have no pain in my leg," I said. Ever since the accident at McDonald's, for thirty-four years, seven months, and sixteen days, my knee had hurt, sometimes less than other times, but it had never been pain-free. Now it didn't hurt. The pain was gone. It was absolutely amazing, a life-changing experience. Although I still have some pain in my upper back, above my fusion surgery, we are addressing that in other ways.

Chapter 18

*L*ife was going great. Just when I thought it was safe to go back in the water...February 2018, I was on a domestic flight. As they announced "Fasten your seat belts" for our descent into Boston, I suddenly felt a blow to the left side of my head and left shoulder. When I opened my eyes, they were filled with stars. A luggage compartment door lay on the floor in the aisle. I couldn't believe it. I was overcome by a throbbing headache and intense pain in my shoulder and neck. A flight attendant came over and laughed as she picked up my hat. She picked up the luggage compartment door and tried to reattach it above my seat. The door did not properly reconnect or fit back into alignment. Denise and I told the attendant we felt it was not safe to have it like that. She laughed and said it was good enough. She went and sat in the jump seat beside another flight attendant, pointed at me, and laughed again. Drago had been lying between my feet facing under the seat in front of me with his head on my foot. He immediately tried to comfort me, pressing his head into my leg. After landing, EMTs saw me and offered to take me to the hospital. I declined because I was tired and wanted to get home. It was late at night and I hoped that I would feel better the next morning and that I'd only have a little bump on my head and a sore shoulder. I couldn't sleep that night because of the pain. Toward morning, I threw up from the relentlessly intense headache and shooting pain in my neck and shoulders. I contacted my doctor and he directed me to the urgent care. I was diagnosed with a severe concussion and whiplash. The incident also caused me to have a subluxed, dislocated right clavicle. Since then, my quality of life has been greatly impacted. I've been dealing with dizziness, balance issues, ringing in my ears, double vision, debilitating headaches, light sensitivity, sleep problems, fatigue, memory issues, and excruciating pain.

This incident caused PTSD symptoms and disturbing flashbacks from clicking noises. I contacted my counselor to work through this experience and injuries, not wanting to let the symptoms fester. My counselor also has had me work to desensitize the powerful flashbacks of clicking noises by using a dog trainer clicker. Hearing the clicker over and over again over the course of months reduced the intensity and frequency of the flashbacks. Part of my treatment has included extensive physical therapy for my headaches, eyes, neck, balance, and clavicle pain. The doctor also prescribed a figure-of-eight brace for me the to wear, hoping it would help. I had to have surgery in November 2018 to re-attach the clavicle. This was a high-risk procedure. A thoracic surgeon and orthopedic surgeon had to perform the surgery. A hole had to be drilled in my sternum and my clavicle, so a wire could reconnect the clavicle to the joint. The pain was intense after surgery and kept me in the hospital for days. Two months post-op, I had complications from the surgery and my clavicle subluxed again, putting me in extreme daily pain. The options to try to help my subluxed clavicle are more involved and a revision surgery has an even higher risk of complications. The pain dominates my life while I also continue to suffer post-concussion syndrome symptoms. The dislocated clavicle continues to be an issue, popping out dozens of times in a single day. I continue to see doctors to try to help deal with these injuries and my new PTSD symptoms. I pray I will heal physically and mentally but don't know to what extent these symptoms will continue to impact my life. I use my "one-base-at-a-time" philosophy to take on these challenges.

A few months later, in June of 2018 I had to confront my new fear of flying and being on an airplane head-on.

My cell phone rang around 1:45 a.m. and our daughter's name appeared on the screen. At the time, Cacky was living in San Diego, where she was studying for her Ph.D in Depth Psychology with an emphasis in Somatic Studies and a specific focus in trauma. As soon as I answered, I heard fear in her voice. My heart sank. Her voice was shaking as she tried to whisper through the phone. Drago sensed the stress and immediately jumped onto the bed to try to distract me and get me to focus on him. Denise woke up as she had a sixth sense something was amiss with one of our daughters and I put my cell on speaker as Cacky described what had happened.

She had called 911 after hearing someone in the hallway outside her condo shouting, "All you fucking cunt bitches in this place are going to see what I'm made of. You're going to pay!" She told us that, when the police arrived, they smelled smoke coming from the condo three doors down and across the hall from her. The police called for the fire department to respond to the scene before knocking on the door repeatedly, announcing that they were police for about thirty minutes. There was no response. They warned that, in two minutes, they would enter. They knocked again. They announced that they were entering. Suddenly, she heard a sudden burst of what sounded like pop-rockets. She didn't realize it was gunfire until she heard the calls of, "Officer down!" The man had shot indiscriminately, spraying bullets through his door and walls into other condos and out into the hallway, hitting both police officers and wounding them. It was the most helpless feeling, knowing my daughter was alone on the other side of the country, on the other side of that hallway, and that I couldn't get to her. I passed the phone to Denise, picked up her cell to call the airlines and booked the next flight to San Diego. I knew there would be stress and that I could face flashbacks on the flight, but I had Drago to help get me through it. I was determined to get to Cacky as soon as possible.

Over the phone, we heard the howling of sirens as every available unit arrived on scene and SWAT helicopters circled overhead. Cacky had been sitting next to the door to the hallway when the gunfire had started but was now in her bedroom doorway. We asked her to move into the kitchen and lie on the floor, hoping it was a safer location. We listened as I paced around through hours of fear and uncertainty, our hearts beating in our throats, terrified of what might happen next. We searched the internet for news as Cacky tried to make out what the SWAT team in the hallway and police outside in the courtyard were saying. She heard officers saying they did not know where the gunman was and instructing residents to shelter in place. People from the neighborhood were posting videos, but they just showed us what the scene looked like outside. Shortly thereafter, we saw the breaking news on multiple stations. Mostly, we just kept talking with Cacky, assuring her that we loved her, as we waited for information. In the background a police dog was barking intensely and Cacky was terrified he might get shot. Finally, the police gave the all clear. The threat was over. The gunman was found dead in his condo.

Drago and I went to the airport. He could sense my anxiety and stayed glued to my side, trying his best to interrupt my stress. Our flight arrived in San Diego and we made it to the condo about twelve hours after it had all begun. We walked straight into an active crime scene with a mobile command center, many police and police cars, and lots of crime tape blocking off streets and sidewalks. It pained me to know that Cacky was still in her condo. The police said they didn't want her to risk cross-contaminating the hallway but told me to find the lead detective. She was wonderful and asked me to call Cacky and tell her they would be in there in five minutes to escort her out to me. I'll never forget seeing her when she exited the building. I wanted to get to her as fast as possible, but I was ordered to stay on the other side of the crime tape as they walked her to me. Once she arrived, I hugged her. I did not want to let her go.

I'm so proud of her for acting quickly and calling 911. Sadly, this wasn't the first time. Cacky had told us about this terrifying neighbor multiple times. How he would simply yell and swear in his condo and act aggressively. There'd been numerous calls to 911, to her landlord and the condo association to express her increasing concern and to say that she was scared of what he might do. She worried that the situation was escalating and all the women in the building were at risk. In the days following the shooting, news reports emerged of his extensive history of mental health problems and violence against women. Neighbors, too, had called 911. There were visits from the police. He'd spent several months in a psychiatric hospital. Even worse, a young woman who ultimately moved out of her condo in fear for her life, said he had once chased her with a knife and also followed her into a Starbucks while threatening to kill her. She was ultimately attacked by him in that same hallway in front of her own unit when he grabbed her by the hair and slammed her head into the floor until she lost consciousness. She suffered a traumatic brain injury and developed PTSD as a result. Still, he was not removed from the complex. And all of that information was sealed.

In advance of Cacky renting this place, I had done intense research through contacts at multiple police departments, with security contractors, and even Navy Seal friends to check to see if this condo and the neighborhood it was in was truly safe. Every one of them reported back that they couldn't find anything in their extensive background checks to suggest any history of problems. In fact, one police officer told me he would let his daughter live there. Before Cacky signed the lease, I asked the landlord numerous times if there was any history of problems with any of the neighbors in the condo or nearby. "Not any crimes," he told me. In fact, he said, they had a part-time security service for added peace of mind, but there were no problems. I felt absolutely horrible that I had failed to find any of this history of crime and terror.

At that moment, however, I was just glad to have Cacky safe in my arms. I thanked whomever and whatever had watched over her. We went to the hotel and Cacky was pretty quiet for a couple of days.

During this time, I reached out to my counselor to proactively address this traumatic experience, not only for me but to see how Denise and I could be of support to Cacky. Everything I'd seen and felt had the potential to become another tentacle of the kraken that is my PTSD, exacerbating it even further. I was intent on keeping my promise to Cacky back in 2010 that I wouldn't give up on counseling and would reach out for help in the face of any new trauma. Taking action at the first sign of crisis was a testament to just how far I'd come in the process of dealing with my PTSD head-on. I did not want this already terrible experience to gain power over me and my family going forward. I know now that it is a sign of strength to ask for help. And I needed to be strong for Cacky as we dealt with the days in front of us.

Over the course of a week, we went back and forth between the hotel and the complex to pick up things Cacky needed. After a couple of days, she started to open up and talk about what had happened. One day, we went back to the condo to retrieve a few more things. Even though it was still an active crime scene and they were continuing their investigation, they let me walk through. A detective escorted me through the hallway to my daughter's unit. I was shocked by the scene. There were evidence markers on the floor and walls pointing to where bullets and bullet casings had been recovered. There were fragments of drywall, and bullet holes riddled the walls. The smell of gunpowder still hung in the air. Many of the doors to the surrounding condo units were broken and smashed in the aftermath because the SWAT team had knocked them down when no one answered during their search for possible victims. Plywood covered some of the most damaged doors. I felt sick to my stomach. It looked like videos I'd seen on TV of war zones. Some of the bullet holes were larger than dimes. I looked through one into the gunman's condo and saw a banner for a website, which I checked later and found that it allowed people to buy guns without serial numbers and kits to construct their own unregistered weapons. It was scary to know he was able to obtain an AR-15 assault rifle and other handguns, especially considering that, in the court case from the previous January, the judge ruled he could not possess any guns.

As I walked toward her condo door, I saw that there was a bullet lodged in the drywall. It was in line, only six inches from where Cacky's head had been when the shooting started, when she was sitting in a chair, her ear pressed to the door trying to hear what the police officers were saying. As I walked up and down the hallway, I saw where the armor piercing bullets he was using had gone through many other walls and multiple wood doors in a row. Yet that bullet was stopped in the drywall by a miracle. Someone must have been watching over her. I said a prayer and thanked God Cacky wasn't physically injured. I pray that she will not be emotionally scarred and suffer the invisible wounds caused by PTSD. I am extremely proud of how she's actively working through this trauma, using this deeply painful, life-changing experience to empower herself not only as a person but also moving forward as a doctor. She has inspired us.

Several police officers and detectives thanked Cacky for having the courage to call 911. They told us that it was very likely that she had prevented a mass shooting. There had been fire alarms set off at the condo complex the previous five nights, and they believed the gunman had been the person who set them off as a rehearsal to study how people left the building because his plan was to shoot them as they exited. They explained that he'd had many boxes of armor piercing bullets in his unit and that he'd been dressed head to toe in body armor. Fortunately, the two police officers shot during the incident had been wounded but would survive.

As we walked to the rental car, Cacky told me that the first officer to check on her said she must have had a guardian angel looking out for her, because it was a miracle she hadn't been shot. Then she told me how she was struck by how much he looked like Terry, everything from his height to his build to his sandy blonde hair, from his tortoise shell glasses to the shape and size of his mustache. She said it was uncanny. I texted Chip to tell him, and he replied, "I believe it must have been him."

Seated inside the car, I reopened Waze on my phone, went to my history, and clicked on the hotel address. Instead of returning us by the route we had come, the app told me to turn left. It seemed odd to me that we were taking a long way around. Then the app directed me to turn right onto Terry Lane. My heart jumped. I looked for a street sign. The spellings were the same. Goosebumps rose on my arms as powerful chills ran through me that, strangely, filled me with warmth. It was the weirdest sensation. A short time later, Waze told us to turn on to Racine Road. Racine is the Wisconsin town in which Terry had lived. I felt like these were signs and not mere coincidence. My faith was strengthened that Terry was with us and had been our guardian Angel. I took a deep breath and internally acknowledged his presence. I told him how much I loved him and thanked him for looking out for Cacky. Drago leaned his head into my shoulder. Terry has always been a source of strength in my life and here was another example of his continued love and support. In our multiple travels to and from the condo complex over the next several days, we used the Waze app every time, but it never sent us on that route again.

Epilogue

*I*t seems impossible. Only nine short years ago, I was wracked by so much physical and emotional pain that I thought there was no way that I could ever be free. I was in despair.

Then I read these words:

> They went off to war brimming with confidence and eager for the fight in Iraq and Afghanistan. They returned, many of them, showing no visible wounds but utterly transformed by combat—with symptoms of involuntary trembling, irritability, restlessness, depression, nightmares, flashbacks, insomnia, emotional numbness, sensitivity to noise, and, all too often, a tendency to seek relief in alcohol, drugs or suicide.

I hadn't gone to war but, as an eighteen-year-old young man, I too had once been "brimming with confidence" and eager to confront the challenges of being an adult. I too had dreams I wanted to pursue. Although I will never equate my experience with that of the soldiers who give so much of themselves, so selflessly, in combat, I too, in my own way, had returned from a traumatic experience and been utterly transformed by it.

Too many times since then, the world had been a frightening place, one that sometimes made me tremble with fear or anxiety, made me lash out in anger or left me exhausted, depressed, numb, unable to sleep, tempted by alcohol, and turned inside out by my fear of flashbacks and nightmares. And still, challenges arise, such as what happened on the flight and in San Diego. Pain will continue to be an issue in my life. Only now, I'm equipped to act quickly and in ways that help reduce the problems rather than exacerbate them.

I had still managed to achieve many of my goals—I had made it to the major leagues, working in the ballpark that occupied my childhood dreams, but it had left me feeling that I had fallen short in the ways that mattered most to me, as a husband to Denise and a father to my two precious girls. Yet I never stopped trying, even as I often failed. I could not run and, at times, I could barely walk, but I kept going, one base at a time, with faith that, one day, somehow, someway, I would find peace and find a way to become the man, husband, and father I wanted to be.

I've struggled with PTSD for over thirty years. For much of that time, I was consumed by guilt, fear, self-loathing, and shame. These symptoms, more than most of the physical pain I have experienced, more than most flashbacks or nightmares, were the worst aspects of PTSD. It wasn't so much the impact it had on me personally, but the impact it had on my family, those I love, and who loved me, in spite of myself.

To all who suffer from PTSD, know this: In spite of it all, today, against all odds, I am making progress. Today, I continue to work toward healing. I may never reach home plate but, for the rest of my life, I will continue to take the same approach that has carried me this far. One step at a time. One base at a time.

When I look at Denise and my daughters, who may never have been a part of my life if not for this ordeal, I feel extremely lucky and blessed. I haven't been alone. Even before I realized it, many others stood beside me. My family and friends and doctors. My friends with the Brewers and the Red Sox and throughout baseball. The groundskeeping community, and all those wonderful people I have met since it became known that I have PTSD—my friends Bob, Joe, Lucas and his friend Jessy, who I never met, but who has been with me ever since I slipped that bracelet bearing his name onto my wrist.

It is never too late to take that first step and I am proud to stand with you, proud to be a PTSD survivor.

Resources

If you are in crisis or know someone in crisis, or are simply in need of guidance and resources for support, please reach out to one of the organizations below. They are here to help.

National Suicide Prevention Lifeline
800-273-TALK (8255)
suicidepreventionlifeline.org

Veterans Crisis Line
800-273-8255, PRESS 1
Text 838255
Crisis chat line confidential: VeteransCrisisLine.net/Chat

HomeBase.org (for veteran and family care)
617-724-5202

US Department of Veterans Affairs
www.va.gov

PTSD: National Center for PTSD
www.ptsd.va.gov/

Acknowledgments

A heartfelt thank you to my incredible wife, Denise, and our amazing daughters for your love and support. This book would not have been possible without your encouragement. You planted the seeds, saying I should write my memoir with the hope that it would help people. Little did I know one of those people would be me. Words can't express the appreciation I feel for your believing in me and us, even during the most challenging struggles. You inspire me. Thank you for not giving up on me or us. I love you!!! XOXO

A big thank you to my mom, Marjorie, and brothers, Chip and Terry, and my son-in-law, Luc Tendron for your love and incredible support.

Special thanks to: Paula Ann and David Pullins, Jason Griffeth, friends and coworkers, the Boston Red Sox, Milwaukee Brewers, and Major League Baseball. Thank you for helping me live my Major League Baseball dream. My job is the next best thing to playing.

I'm grateful to Glenn Stout for your compassion, encouragement, many hours of listening, and working with me to write this book. You are absolutely fantastic to work with. Thank you to Dawn Oberg and Saorla Stout for transcribing the interview tapes.

I'm appreciative of Kevin Balfe, Anthony Ziccardi, Jacob Hoye, and the great Post Hill Press publishing team for believing in my story and all of your support in bringing my book to publication.

Thank you, Paul Sennott of Sennott, Rogers and Williams LLP for your guidance and support.

Thank you, Billie Weiss, for making time and extra efforts to take the cover photo.

A special thank-you to Buster Olney for writing the foreword and for sharing my story on ESPN E:60 May 2013 "Fenway's Keeper" feature to bring awareness to PTSD. I'll always remember when we first met, speaking only for a couple minutes before light rain started during BP for a Yankees versus Red Sox game. I was truly humbled when you reached out a few weeks later to ask if you could share my story to help inspire others. Your vision touched many lives and also helped bring this book to market. I also want to thank producer Heather Lombardo for your compassion and contributions with the making of the ESPN E:60 feature. Thank you, Jennifer Chafitz. I'm humbled and grateful for your vision and compassion helping create the ESPN Sports Center feature Oct. 2018 "Dave and Drago" to raise awareness of PTSD and detail how amazing service dogs are. The response from both of these features has been incredibly heart-warming and powerful. They are inspiring many more people than we will ever know.

A huge thank-you to the too-numerous-to-mention medical professionals who helped me through my challenges. I figure forty-five surgeries are better than forty-six. I appreciate all your skills in helping me heal physically and emotionally.

Thank you to everyone who makes the choice and time to read my book. I hope you are inspired to celebrate life and make the most of every day, because you never know when the next challenge will happen.

To Drago, thank you for being an outstanding partner and service dog. I love you!

About the Author

*D*avid R. Mellor is the Senior Director of Grounds for the Boston Red Sox Baseball team at Fenway Park where he oversees everything that involves the playing field, from games and events to field maintenance.

As the leading innovator of elaborate patterns used on athletic turf and turf in general, articles about David's work have been published in *The New York Times* and *USA Today* and he has appeared on numerous television and radio programs including ESPN's E:60 Fenway Keeper, the TODAY show, CBS Sunday Morning, and WEEI Sports Radio. His mowing patterns have been featured in the American Folk Art Museum and an international art exhibit. David has published two books on gardening and horticulture, *Picture Perfect: Mowing Techniques for Lawns, Landscapes, and Sports* (Hardcover, Wiley, 2001), and *The Lawn Bible: How to Keep It Green, Groomed, and Growing Every Season of the Year* (Paperback, Hyperion, 2003), both of which continue to be bestsellers in Amazon. com's Home & Garden category. *Picture Perfect* is considered the text book for lawn patterns. He has co-authored or contributed to eleven other books.

David has cared for some of the greenest lawns in the nation—the ballparks used by the California Angels, San Francisco Giants, Green Bay Packers, Milwaukee Brewers, and, of course, the Boston Red Sox for eighteen years. He has thirty-four seasons of Major League Baseball experience during which he also worked eight years for the Green Bay Packers' games at Milwaukee's County Stadium.

David considers himself one of the luckiest people in the world, living by the old baseball saying, *"one base at a time."* He buys a lottery ticket anytime the jackpot rises over one hundred million dollars as the statistics of winning millions of dollars is more likely than the chance of being hit by two different cars in two different cities.